INTERNSHIP ROADMAP:
MAPPING OUT YOUR PATH TO PROFESSIONAL SUCCESS

BY
RAVI ARORA

Preface

The book's title speaks for itself, and I chose it this way on purpose. It lets people know exactly what they're getting when they pick it up. This is my first book, my first attempt to put my experiences into words, and I'm doing it to share them with students all over the world. So, thank you for choosing my book. I really appreciate it. Welcome to **"Internship Roadmap: Mapping Out Your Path to Professional Success."** This book is for everyone, but it particularly addresses challenges that students commonly face during internship.

It's a book that everyone should read. Parents might find it helpful to read, especially if their child is about to start their first internship. And for aspiring students looking to begin their career journey, this book is important to read beforehand. If you're in charge of a school, college, or any educational institution, this book is crucial for you. It helps you grasp the latest insights into internships and guides you on how to ensure your students succeed during their internship programs. This book is equally important for organizations. If you're responsible for arranging internship programs at your company, recruiting interns, and overseeing their time with you, this book is a must-read. It shows you how to set up a successful internship experience and create an environment where interns can make the most of their time with your company.

Undoubtedly, an internship presents a wonderful chance for all students, not only for individual growth but also for professional advancement. However, there are numerous challenges that students often face during this journey. My book is aimed at turning those challenges into positive and successful experiences. Think of this book as your reliable guide from the very beginning of planning your internship to transforming it into a potential long-term career opportunity. It's like having a trusted companion by your side, offering insights not just on how to navigate through the process, but also on handling common difficulties you might encounter during your internship and how to conquer them.

This book holds significant importance because, prior to an internship, much of what you learn from books is theoretical. While you gather a lot of knowledge, it might be unclear how to apply that knowledge in real-world situations or practical scenarios. This book bridges that gap and shows you how your theoretical understanding transforms into practical experience in the real world.

You might still wonder, "Why should I read this book? I already know a lot about internships." Indeed, you do, but this book goes beyond what you might have heard from others. It helps you understand internships in a broader sense. You'll learn about the various types of internships available for students. Don't limit yourself to the traditional idea of a Summer Internship. The concept has evolved, and remote and international internships are now widely recognized as well.

You should definitely read this book if you're uncertain about how to apply for internships, if you want to excel during your internship, or if you're seeking guidance on how to make the most of your internship for your future career opportunities.

By the time you finish reading this book, I am sure you'll have a solid grasp of why internships are so important. You'll also see how they align with your career goals. The guidance in this book will prepare you well for your internship journey. It will help you not only navigate your internship successfully but also extract the most from the experience. This will make you a confident and capable candidate, ready to apply for relevant professional jobs in any organization.

Keep in mind that an internship isn't just a short-term task for your college requirement. It holds value beyond that. Think of it as an investment in your learning, efforts, and future. By reading this book, you'll gain the knowledge to confidently navigate the internship world and turn this experience into a journey of job opportunities. I hope you find this book enjoyable and insightful.

Thank You

Table of Contents

UNDERSTANDING INTERNSHIPS 7

INTRODUCTION TO INTERNSHIPS AND PROFESSIONAL SUCCESS 22

NAVIGATING THE SUMMER INTERNSHIP LANDSCAPE 47

EXPLORING INTERNATIONAL INTERNSHIP OPPORTUNITIES 82

THRIVING IN REMOTE INTERNSHIPS 105

MAXIMIZING YOUR PROFESSIONAL GROWTH DURING INTERNSHIPS 120

OVERCOMING CHALLENGES AND OBSTACLES IN INTERNSHIPS 135

TRANSITIONING FROM INTERNSHIP TO FULL-TIME EMPLOYMENT 151

DESIGNING YOUR OWN PATH: SELF-DEFINED INTERNSHIP JOURNEY 177

CREATING A LONG-TERM CAREER DEVELOPMENT PLAN 209

ADDITIONAL RESOURCES FOR INTERNSHIP SUCCESS 228

THANK YOU 239

Chapter 1

Understanding Internships

Right from the start, I really liked learning new things. I enjoyed reading many books, articles, and magazines. Different authors who wrote about their real-life experiences in a way that inspired others caught my attention. They shared their stories to help people learn from them. This passion for learning has always motivated me. Nowadays, even with technology, I still believe books are very important medium to communicate and express the thoughts. I also think that writing about experiences in a book is a great way to connect with many people. So, I decided to share my own story and the things I've learned from living in different countries and meeting lots of talented people around the world.

I decided to write, but figuring out what to write about was a big question, especially for someone like me who is a new author. I didn't want to write only about myself. I wanted to address the problems I've faced and the problems people around me are dealing with. I realized that many others might also face similar issues in the future. So, I looked around to find a topic that would really touch my emotions. It's not just about me; it's about how I can make a positive impact on others' lives.

Deciding the subject for my book was a challenge since I had a wide range of experiences and I always feel like to share my knowledge and learning with others, focusing on a topic that is common and faced by everyone at some point in their professional career. After much thought, I realized that the area of internships was not taken seriously during my time. Academic institutes were not dedicated to providing proper guidelines or practices, and students faced numerous challenges without knowing how to get the right help.

I have strong opinion about education system, from the early classes to higher education. I believe that our education system needs a lot of modernization or maybe a different approach. So, I thought about picking a topic related to this bigger change in the education system and sharing my perspective on it.

So, I chose to write about internships. It's a topic that doesn't often get the attention it deserves, neither in academic institutions nor in workplaces, even though it's a big concern for many students. Almost every student encounter challenges during their internships, and I wanted to talk about my experiences and offer ways to make internships better for them.

My book will primarily focus on students because I am deeply concerned about their professional careers and their aspirations to secure a good internship. Students from reputable universities or colleges often have an edge or advantage in getting internships in top-grade work environments, which may lead to excellent job opportunities based on their internship outcomes. However, You also want to acknowledge that there are millions of students who do not have the same level of privilege and opportunities. I want to use my experience and the experiences shared by my friends and colleagues to help these students secure their desired internships.

Let's start from the basics, understanding what internships are, and then gradually progress towards how to secure a good internship and deliver it successfully. We'll explore the steps needed to achieve this and make a positive impact on the internship program for all students.

Understanding Internship

It's a bit unfair and unfortunate that many organizations expect college students to have work experience when they're primarily focused on studying or perhaps working part-time to support themselves. Even though you're seeking your first job, the competitive job market makes it tough to stand out if you're only concentrating on your studies and lack work experience. This is where internships come into play. Understanding their importance is crucial.

An internship typically lasts around 2 to 3 months and offers you an opportunity to work in a real-world setting. This experience is vital as it provides your first step into the professional world. If you don't take internships seriously, you might regret it later. Many students find it challenging to secure a job directly without any work experience. This message is directed at those students who are in a situation where they lack work experience and find it difficult to secure a job. Sometimes, internships don't directly lead to a job, but they still contribute to your growth and learning. It's important to consider internships as stepping stones to your future career.

Welcome to the world of internships - a short-term work experience that opens doors to valuable learning opportunities, practical skills development, and a chance to make a lasting impression on potential employers. With an internship, you can bridge the gap between theoretical knowledge and real-world application, setting yourself up for success in your chosen career path.

An internship offers college students and recent graduates the chance to gain practical knowledge and skills in a specific field or industry. It's not just about textbooks; internships provide real-world experience that can enhance your resume and help you stand out in a competitive job market. Start your journey towards a successful career with an internship today.

A Thorough Exploration

Embarking on an internship can be an exciting and transformative experience for college graduates, as it opens doors to a world of possibilities and growth. In this book, we will delve into the valuable opportunities that internships present and take a comprehensive exploration of each aspect to help you make the most of this crucial phase in your professional journey.

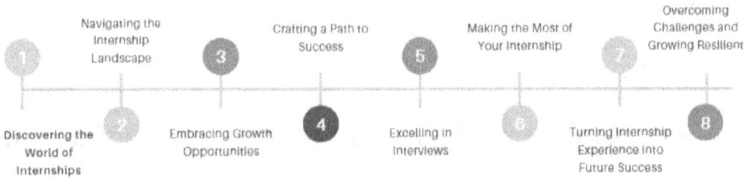

Discovering the World of Internships: Internships are more than just temporary positions; they are stepping stones to success. By participating in an internship, you gain first-hand exposure to the real-world application of your academic knowledge. This practical experience allows you to bridge the gap between theory and practice, enhancing your understanding of the industry and profession you've chosen. We will probe into the multifaceted benefits of internships, helping you grasp how they shape your career path and personal development.

Navigating the Internship Landscape: Understanding the types of internships available and finding the one that aligns with your interests and aspirations can be a challenging task. Whether it's a summer internship, a part-time commitment during the academic year, or the choice between a paid or unpaid opportunity, we will guide you through the decision-making process. We'll provide strategies for discovering internship opportunities that match your goals and share tips on standing out during the application process.

Embracing Growth Opportunities: Internships are learning experiences, and they offer a fertile ground for skill development. In the upcoming chapters, we'll dive deep into the essential skills that internships cultivate, such as effective communication, problem-solving, adaptability, and teamwork. You'll learn how to make the most of the mentorship and guidance available during your internship, fostering personal and professional growth throughout your journey.

Crafting a Path to Success: Preparation is key to making the most of your internship experience. We'll provide practical advice on creating a standout resume and crafting a compelling cover letter that highlights your strengths and achievements. You'll discover how to tap into your network to uncover hidden internship opportunities and gain insights into tailoring your application to different companies and industries.

Excelling in Interviews: Interviews can be nerve-wracking, but we've got you covered. We'll equip you with the best practices and strategies to excel in internship interviews, from preparing effectively to showcasing your skills and enthusiasm. By the end of this chapter, you'll feel confident and well-prepared to shine in any interview scenario.

Making the Most of Your Internship: Once you secure the internship, the journey continues. We'll explore the art of setting meaningful goals for your internship and provide guidance on navigating the workplace dynamics. You'll learn how to build strong professional relationships, handle challenges with grace, and embrace new learning opportunities that arise during your internship tenure.

Turning Internship Experience into Future Success: An internship is not just a temporary endeavour; it's an investment in your future career. We'll discuss how to leverage your internship experience to open doors to new opportunities. From requesting recommendations and references to positioning yourself for potential full-time job offers, we'll show you how to make your internship a launchpad for future success.

Overcoming Challenges and Growing Resilient: Every journey comes with its share of challenges. In this book, we'll address common internship hurdles and offer strategies for overcoming them. You'll learn the art of resilience, transforming setbacks into stepping stones towards personal and professional growth.

Embracing the Internship Journey: As you navigate through the chapters of this book, you'll be equipped with the knowledge, insights, and confidence to seize the opportunities that internships present. We are dedicated to supporting you in every step of your internship journey, ensuring that you can make informed decisions, embrace growth, and carve a fulfilling path to professional success.

So, let's embark on this transformative adventure together as we unravel the world of internships, empowering you to create a roadmap for a promising and rewarding career.

From Theory to Practice

It's hard to land a job without any practical experience in your field. Most employers require some level of experience, which can be challenging for college students or recent graduates. You've spent years studying and preparing for your career, but without real-world experience, it can be difficult to prove your abilities and stand out from the competition. An internship is the perfect solution to gain the practical knowledge and skills needed to kick-start your career. It provides hands-on experience, networking opportunities, and a chance to apply what you've learned in a real work environment. With an internship, you can bridge the gap between education and employment, making you a more attractive candidate to future employers.

We'll have to navigate different processes and manage many things before beginning the internship. However, before we kickstart this journey, it is essential to comprehend the challenges that come beforehand. It is crucial to know what these challenges are and how we can address them effectively. This part of the chapter holds utmost significance as it helps us understand and mitigate these challenges. I am confident that many of you may have faced or will face these challenges, so it's vital not to ignore this important section of our chapter. Let's dive in and explore these challenges, knowing the reality and finding ways to overcome them.

Getting a great internship can be tough for college students because they have to deal with different challenges while trying to succeed in their professional journey.

Don't be discouraged by these challenges. I've shared some of the top challenges that came to my mind, but in reality, there could be many more, and some might be specific to your situation. However, it's essential to prepare for them in advance.

Lack of Guidance: This is one of my best reasons for writing this book. Back in my time, there was a lack of proper guidance available on internships. People didn't fully understand the purpose of internships and where this could lead to. Nowadays, with the abundance of information on the internet and social media, things have changed, but still, many people remain confused and misinformed. While you may receive plenty of free advice, only a few can provide you with the right guidance. Be prepared for that.

Limited Work Experience: Many students face the challenge of limited or no prior work experience. Without relevant professional experience, it can be challenging to stand out among other internship applicants.

Competitive Job Market: The job market is highly competitive, and securing a great internship requires a strong application and interview strategy to differentiate oneself from other candidates.

Unclear Career Goals: Some students struggle to define their career goals, which makes it difficult to target specific internships that align with their interests and aspirations.

Lack of Networking: Building a professional network is vital for finding internship opportunities. Students who have not actively networked may face difficulties in discovering relevant openings.

Resume and Cover Letter Preparation: Crafting an effective resume and cover letter that highlights skills and achievements can be challenging for students who may have limited experience in job application procedures.

Difficulty in Finding Opportunities: Locating internships that match one's field of study or career goals can be daunting, especially when there is a lack of awareness about available opportunities.

Financial Constraints: Some internships are unpaid, and students may face financial challenges if they need to support themselves while working in an unpaid or low-paid position.

Lack of Interview Skills: Students who have not had prior interview experience may struggle to present themselves confidently and effectively during internship interviews.

Balancing Academic Commitments: Juggling internship applications and interviews with academic responsibilities can be stressful, as students need to manage their time effectively.

Limited Industry Knowledge: Lack of familiarity with the specific industries or companies they are applying to may lead to difficulties in articulating why they are the right fit for the internship.

Each of these challenges requires a thoughtful approach and proactive measures to overcome. By addressing these obstacles head-on, students can increase their chances of landing a great internship and setting themselves up for future success in their chosen career paths.

To overcome the challenges students, face in landing a great internship, it is essential to adopt proactive measures and take deliberate steps to enhance their prospects. Throughout the upcoming chapters, we will explore in-depth the right approaches, methods, and strategies to address each obstacle effectively.

One major challenge students encounter is the lack of work experience or a limited professional background. To combat this, students can seek relevant opportunities such as part-time jobs, volunteering, or campus activities that align with their career interests. Building practical experience will bolster their resumes and make them more appealing to potential internship providers.

In a competitive job market, standing out from the crowd is crucial. In the forthcoming chapters, we will delve into techniques for optimizing resume content, crafting compelling cover letters, and emphasizing transferable skills to make a persuasive case as an internship candidate.

Clarifying career goals is essential for targeting the right internships. Through self-reflection and career exploration, students can gain clarity about their aspirations. We will guide readers in defining their career objectives and finding internships that align with their passions and long-term goals.

Networking plays a pivotal role in internship success. In the upcoming chapters, we will explore various in-person and online networking strategies to help students connect with industry professionals and discover hidden internship opportunities.

Mastering interview skills is vital for impressing potential employers. Our forthcoming chapters will focus on interview preparation, providing students with tips and practice scenarios to enhance their confidence and performance during internship interviews.

Discovering relevant internship opportunities can be challenging, but we will equip students with various channels and resources to find internships that match their fields of study and interests. Financial constraints can deter some students from pursuing internships, especially unpaid or low-paid ones. We will discuss ways to navigate such challenges, such as seeking scholarship programs or part-time work opportunities to support their internship pursuits.

Balancing academic commitments with internship pursuits is a common challenge. Our upcoming chapters will provide time management techniques and effective planning methods to help students optimize their schedules.

Finally, strengthening industry knowledge is crucial for demonstrating genuine interest during interviews and applications. Our upcoming chapters will emphasize the importance of researching industries and companies to increase students' chances of securing the right internship.

By applying the strategies outlined throughout this book, students will be well-prepared to overcome these challenges and maximize their chances of securing a great internship. Each next chapter will offer detailed insights, practical advice, and actionable steps to empower students to take control of their internship journey and pave the way for a successful and fulfilling career ahead.

"Believe you can, and you're halfway there."

- *Theodore Roosevelt*

Chapter 2

Introduction to Internships and Professional Success

Understanding the Importance of Internships

Understanding the importance of internships is crucial for college graduates. In my experience, I have come across many stories from friends, relatives, and acquaintances who have done internships but didn't gain much from them. Some of them even interned at big corporations but couldn't secure good jobs afterward. On the contrary, there are those who did internships at smaller organizations but successfully landed great jobs.

The market holds a myth that interning at a big corporate guarantee a bright future, but the reality is different. It doesn't matter if you intern at a large or small company, in any location or industry. What truly matters is what you do during your internship, the experiences you gain, and the value you bring. Your internship and the value you create drive the course of your future career.

Blaming students alone is not fair for the myth because our traditional approach here has always been the same. During our college or university days, we have a semester dedicated to internships, but we are often provided with limited guidance. We end up applying for various internships based on our own criteria for success and eventually land one without even knowing if that is right one.

However, since we are not properly told or guided about what to do during the internship, we complete it without gaining much value. As a result, after the internship, hundreds and thousands of students struggle to secure good jobs. It could be because of their approach towards the internship, the methods they used to execute it, the environment they were in during the internship, or even their lack of seriousness towards it.

Let me illustrate the importance of internships with an example. Consider a recent college graduate named Philip. He decided to do an internship at a local Water Distribution Company. During the application process, he convinced the company that he could handle the responsibilities of the internship. They agreed, and Philip started his internship.

In the beginning, for the first 10 days, he didn't receive much attention, and it wasn't until the next 15-20 days that someone finally assigned him some small tasks. Unfortunately, nobody explained the significance of these tasks, as the company often believes that internships provide little value due to their short duration.

In Philip's case, he was given the task of tracking the empty water bottles coming into the warehouse and recording where they were being sent, whether to local shops, offices, or houses. His job was to ensure that no water bottles were missed in the process.

Philip diligently performed his tasks, counting and tracking the water bottles. He would create daily reports and even crafted a nice dashboard to showcase his work during his two-month internship. He learned about the entire steps of checking, receiving, and tracking the empty bottles, canes and containers.

After successfully completing his internship, Philip likely received a nice certificate from his supervisor, acknowledging his hard work and completion of the internship. However, the harsh reality is that despite doing well in his project and receiving a decent score, it didn't really help him land the right job in the market. His internship experience was limited to counting and tracking empty bottles, which didn't contribute much to his career prospects.

Philip missed out on a valuable opportunity during his internship. Instead of just completing the required tasks, he could have taken a more proactive approach to understand the entire functioning of the water distribution company. By delving into the flow of information from the order to delivery and dealing with empty bottles, he could have gained valuable insights and enhanced his internship experience.

The question arises, why didn't he take this approach? Perhaps he was not fully aware of the potential benefits or was not guided properly throughout the internship. Maybe he lacked the motivation or hunger to excel and secure a good job. Whatever the reason, the truth remains that he could have utilized this internship to gain a deeper understanding of the corporate world, which would have been beneficial during his first job interview.

Understanding the internship process is crucial for your professional growth. Now, let's address how Philip could have approached his internship differently in the same company.

Firstly, it's essential to recognize that when you join a corporate office as an intern, they may not immediately assign significant tasks. The company has its own priorities and responsibilities to handle. So, instead of expecting immediate attention, take the initiative to understand the company's operations. Gather information about the water distribution company, such as its offices, franchises, and distribution across various cities. You can also research publicly available information about the company to gain more insights.

By proactively learning about the company's workings, you can be better prepared to contribute effectively during your internship. This knowledge will set you apart and demonstrate your genuine interest in understanding the corporate world.

The second important step is to conduct thorough research on the water distribution industry. Understand the various water distribution models in the market and the entire value chain of the water distribution process. Identify the leading companies in this sector and delve into their operations.

Ask yourself important questions and seek answers through research and analysis. Within 7 to 8 days, you can acquire valuable knowledge about different water distribution companies, their value chains, and their specific areas of expertise. This will give you a strong perspective and help you identify the areas of interest you'd like to explore.

Suppose you have a specialization in sales. In that case, you should focus on understanding the water distribution companies' value chains from a sales perspective. Determine where the sales function fits into this value chain and how it contributes to the overall process.

By conducting this in-depth research, you'll not only gain valuable insights but also position yourself as a knowledgeable and valuable intern in the eyes of the company you are interning with.

Once you have explored the different functions within the sales department of the water distribution company, you'll discover various roles and responsibilities. Some employees are involved in direct sales, while others handle sales calls, on-ground sales, sales strategy, or support sales promotion activities. The specific tasks depend on the company's size and structure.

After identifying the area that interests you the most, the next step is to understand the challenges and business issues faced by the water distribution company in their sales model. Conduct comprehensive market research and study similar industry problems to gain a broader perspective.

Now that you have a clear understanding of the market and the water distribution value chain, you can analyze the specific challenges and problem statements that these companies encounter. Use this information to formulate your unique point of view. Let the company know that you are passionate about the specific sales function and eager to work on addressing these challenges. Express your willingness to collaborate with their team, both on-ground and in the back office, to understand the entire sales process better. By showcasing your research and enthusiasm, you can impress the company and demonstrate your commitment to making a valuable contribution during your internship.

Now, as you add value to the company, the supervisor who will oversee your work will be thrilled to have you onboard. They will provide you with ample opportunities because they see that you truly understand their problems. Even if you come up with potential solutions in the three months of your internship, it doesn't matter if those solutions are immediately implemented or require additional investment. The key is to work on finding short-term and long-term solutions and present them respectfully.

You may find that your quick solutions don't demand any major changes or investments; sometimes, it's about tweaking rules or processes. By doing so, you are solving a real problem for the company and truly adding value. When you later present this entire experience as part of your internship project during a job interview, you'll realize that you have excelled compared to the initial example we discussed.

With this valuable experience and knowledge, you'll confidently share what you accomplished, why you did it, and how you did it. Interviewers will be amazed by your skills, experience, and determination in making a significant impact in just three months. This preparation and success will set you apart and position you well for your future endeavours.

Now, we've covered good example for learning purposes. Let's focus on some key insights that will help you make the most out of your internship. We'll explore the importance of delving deep into the concept, understanding the theory, and applying it practically during your internship.

For students interested in internships, whether it be summer internships, international internships, or remote internships, it is crucial to understand the importance of these opportunities. Internships offer invaluable experiences that can shape your future career trajectory and provide a competitive edge in the job market. This subchapter aims to highlight the significance of internships and why they should be an integral part of your professional journey.

First and foremost, internships provide real-world exposure and practical skills that cannot be obtained solely through classroom education. They allow you to apply theoretical knowledge in a professional environment, bridging the gap between academic learning and practical application. By working alongside industry professionals, you gain insights into the day-to-day workings of your chosen field, enabling you to develop a deeper understanding of its challenges and opportunities. This hands-on experience is highly valued by employers, as it demonstrates your ability to adapt to the demands of the job.

Summer internships, in particular, offer a unique chance to gain concentrated experience during the break from academic studies. These internships often last for a shorter duration, but they provide intense learning opportunities that can significantly enhance your skills and expand your professional network. They also allow you to explore different industries and roles, helping you narrow down your career interests and make informed decisions about your future.

International internships offer an additional layer of benefits. They provide a global perspective, exposing you to different cultures, work practices, and business environments. Through these experiences, you develop cross-cultural communication skills, adaptability, and a broader worldview. Employers increasingly value candidates with international exposure, as it demonstrates flexibility and the ability to work in diverse teams.

In today's digital age, remote internships have gained immense popularity. These internships allow you to work from anywhere, breaking down geographical barriers and opening up opportunities on a global scale. Remote internships offer flexibility, allowing you to balance work and personal commitments while gaining valuable experience. They also foster independence, self-discipline, and time management skills, which are highly sought after in the modern professional landscape.

Let's now explore some important points that highlight the significance of internships. While reading these points, I recommend keeping in mind the examples I mentioned earlier. This will provide you with the right perspective to better grasp their importance.

The Value of Practical Experience:

Practical experience holds immense value for college students, as it bridges the gap between theoretical knowledge gained in the classroom and real-world application. Textbooks and lectures provide essential foundations, but internships offer a unique opportunity to apply that knowledge in a professional setting. Engaging in practical tasks, problem-solving, and decision-making during internships equips students with invaluable skills that cannot be fully attained through academic study alone. By experiencing the actual challenges and intricacies of their chosen field, students gain a deeper understanding of industry practices, which enhances their competence and adaptability as future professionals.

How Internships Complement Academic Learning:

Internships act as a vital complement to academic learning, providing a dynamic and hands-on extension of classroom education. While formal education imparts essential theories and concepts, internships enable students to witness these theories in action and observe their direct impact on real projects and business operations. Working alongside experienced professionals exposes students to industry best practices, innovative technologies, and current trends, enriching their understanding and sharpening their skills. This synergy between academic knowledge and practical experience fosters a well-rounded educational journey, preparing students to face real-world challenges with confidence and competence.

The Impact of Internships on Employability:

Internships play a pivotal role in enhancing employability and career prospects for students. Employers consistently seek candidates with practical experience, and internships provide students with a competitive advantage in the job market. Having an internship on one's resume demonstrates initiative, commitment, and the ability to apply knowledge in a real-world context, which is highly attractive to potential employers. Additionally, internships allow students to build a professional network and gain references from experienced mentors, both of which are valuable assets during job searches. As students complete internships, they develop a portfolio of accomplishments and experiences that elevate their employability, making them stand out as desirable candidates in a competitive job landscape.

In summary, internships play a vital role in your professional development. Whether it's a summer internship, international internship, or remote internship, these experiences offer practical skills, industry exposure, and networking opportunities that can propel your career forward. By understanding the importance of internships and actively seeking out these opportunities, you are laying a solid foundation for your future success.

Benefits of Internships for Students and Interns

Internships are an essential stepping stone towards professional success for students and interns, offering a plethora of valuable benefits. Whether it is a summer internship, an international internship, or a remote internship, these opportunities provide a unique and practical learning experience that cannot be replicated within the confines of a classroom. In this subchapter, we will explore the numerous advantages that internships offer to students and interns, regardless of their niche or specialization.

First and foremost, internships provide real-world exposure and hands-on experience in a specific industry or field. This experience allows students to apply the knowledge they have gained in their academic studies to real-life situations, enhancing their understanding and competence. By working alongside professionals, interns have the opportunity to observe and learn from seasoned experts, gaining insights into industry practices, trends, and the overall professional environment.

Skill Development:

Internships also help students develop and refine their skills. Whether it is communication, problem-solving, teamwork, or time management, internships provide a fertile ground for honing these essential soft skills that are highly sought after by employers. Through practical experience and exposure to real-life challenges, interns develop confidence in their abilities, which translates into better career prospects.

In addition to skill development, internships offer a chance to explore different career paths and industries. By immersing themselves in a particular work environment, students and interns can gain valuable insights into their own preferences and interests. This self-discovery process helps them make informed decisions about their future career choices, ensuring they pursue a path that aligns with their passion and strengths.

Competitive Advantage:

Internships provide a competitive advantage in a fiercely competitive job market. Employers value candidates with relevant work experience, and internships provide just that. By having internships on their resumes, students and interns demonstrate their commitment, initiative, and ability to adapt to professional settings, making them more attractive candidates to potential employers.

Gaining Hands-On Experience:

Internships offer a golden opportunity for college students and recent graduates to gain hands-on experience in their chosen fields. Rather than just studying theories and concepts, interns actively participate in real work projects, tasks, and challenges. This practical experience allows them to see how their academic knowledge translates into real-world applications, giving them a more profound understanding of their profession. Through internships, students can develop critical skills and competencies, learning to navigate complexities, solve problems, and make informed decisions in professional settings.

Building a Professional Network:

Internships open doors to building a valuable and diverse professional network. As interns collaborate with experienced professionals, they establish connections that can prove beneficial throughout their careers. Networking during internships enables students to interact with industry experts, mentors, and potential employers. These relationships can offer valuable guidance, mentorship, and even lead to future job opportunities. By actively engaging with their colleagues and supervisors, interns create lasting connections that enhance their professional growth and open doors to new possibilities.

Clarifying Career Goals:

Internships serve as an excellent platform for college students and recent graduates to clarify their career goals. By immersing themselves in real work environments, interns gain exposure to various roles and industries. This firsthand experience allows them to assess their interests, strengths, and passions, helping them refine their career aspirations. Whether confirming their initial career choice or exploring new directions, internships provide crucial insights that guide students towards making informed decisions about their future paths.

Enhancing Resume and Employability:

Participating in internships significantly enhances students' resumes and employability. Employers value candidates with practical experience, and internships provide tangible evidence of a student's commitment to their chosen profession. Internship experiences demonstrate initiative, motivation, and the ability to apply knowledge in practical situations. Additionally, internships equip students with valuable skills and accomplishments that make them more attractive to potential employers. A well-rounded resume that showcases internship experiences can set students apart in a competitive job market, increasing their chances of landing their desired roles.

Internships offer an array of benefits to students, regardless of their niche or specialization. From gaining real-world exposure and practical skills to building professional connections and exploring career paths, internships are an invaluable investment in one's professional future. Whether it is a summer internship, an international internship, or a remote internship, these opportunities pave the way to professional success and provide a solid foundation for a fulfilling career.

Exploring Different Types of Internships

In today's competitive job market, internships have become an essential stepping stone for students and interns to gain valuable industry experience and enhance their professional skills. Whether you are considering a summer internship, an international internship, or a remote internship, this subchapter will provide you with a comprehensive overview of the different types of internships available.

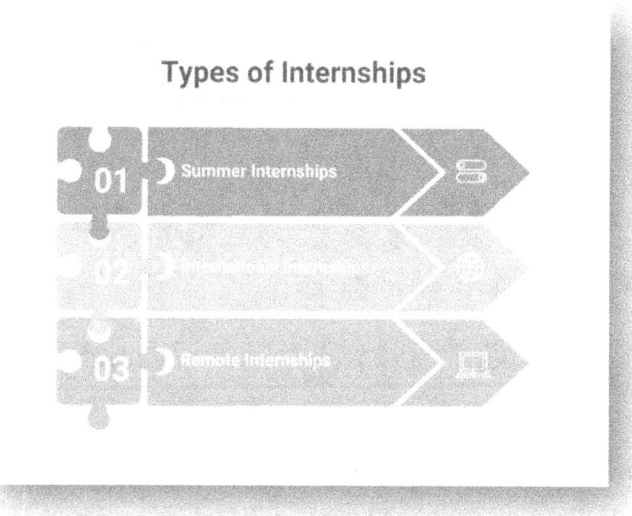

Summer Internships:

Summer internships are a popular choice among students looking to make the most of their summer break. These internships typically last for a few months and offer a hands-on experience in a specific field or industry. They provide an opportunity to apply classroom knowledge in a real-world setting, make professional connections, and explore potential career paths.

1. **International Internships:**

International internships offer a unique chance to gain cross-cultural experience while developing professional skills. These internships allow students to work in a foreign country, immersing themselves in a different culture and expanding their global network. International internships offer the opportunity to learn about different work environments, adapt to new challenges, and develop a global mindset.

2. **Remote Internships:**

Remote internships have gained popularity in recent years, especially with the rise of remote work. These internships allow students to work from any location, eliminating the need for geographical limitations. Remote internships offer flexibility and independence, enabling individuals to balance their academic commitments while gaining practical experience. They also provide an opportunity to develop strong time management and communication skills.

Now, here comes another exciting type of internship that I like to call "**Self-defined Internship**" You must be wondering, "What is this? I haven't heard of it before!" Well, don't worry, we're going to dive deep into this type of internship and discuss why it's so crucial to have such a program. I'll keep you curious for now and save the details for later in the book, but trust me, it's going to be worth the wait! So, let's continue on our journey to uncover the secrets of a successful internship roadmap!

Don't feel overwhelmed by the various names and types of internships you may come across. In different institutes or universities, they might be referred to by different names like campus projects, apprenticeships, semester programs, or semester training. However, for our discussion here, we will mainly focus on four broad and commonly understood types.

Regardless of the type of internship you choose, it is crucial to select one that aligns with your career goals and interests. Researching and identifying internship opportunities that offer relevant experiences and learning opportunities will maximize the benefits of your internship experience.

It is also important to note that internships vary in terms of compensation and duration. Some internships may offer a stipend, while others may be unpaid. Additionally, internships can range from a few weeks to several months, depending on the organization and industry.

By exploring different types of internships, students and interns can gain a broader perspective of the professional world while building a strong foundation for their future careers. Remember, internships are not only about acquiring specific skills but also about personal growth, networking, and discovering your passion. So, embrace the opportunity, be proactive in your search, and embark on your internship journey with enthusiasm and determination.

Setting Goals for Your Internship Journey

Welcome to the exciting part of our journey! You might be thinking, "Whoa, these things are new to me, it sounds challenging!" But don't worry, it's all about setting the right goals for yourself and defining your own unique path.

Life is full of adventures, and to make the most of it, you need to know where you're heading. Setting the right goals and defining your journey is the key to unlocking your true potential. So, get ready to embark on a thrilling ride because this chapter holds the secrets that will benefit you in the long run. Let's dive in and explore the art of defining your own internship journey!

Embarking on an internship journey can be an exciting and transformative experience for students and interns. Whether you are pursuing a summer internship, an international internship, or a remote internship, it is crucial to set clear goals to make the most out of this opportunity and pave your path to professional success. This subchapter will guide you through the process of setting goals for your internship journey and help you unlock your full potential.

The first step in setting goals is self-reflection. Take some time to understand your strengths, weaknesses, and interests. Reflect on what you hope to gain from your internship experience and the skills you want to develop. By identifying your aspirations and areas for growth, you can set goals that align with your personal and professional ambitions.

Next, consider the specific aspects of your internship that you want to focus on. Are you interested in expanding your network, gaining industry knowledge, or enhancing your technical skills? By pinpointing these areas, you can create goals that are tailored to your internship experience and maximize your learning opportunities.

When setting goals, it is important to make them **SMART**: specific, measurable, achievable, realistic, and time-bound.

SMART METHOD

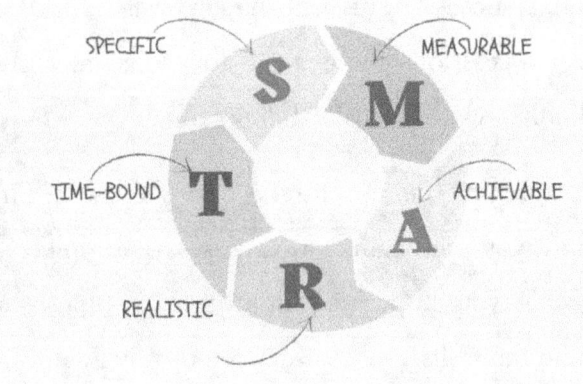

(For those who are unfamiliar with the concept of "Smart Method Theory," I would like to explain it to you. It is a framework that provides a practical and clear way to define your goals and objectives. By using this approach, you can increase your chances of successfully achieving your targets. "Smart" stands for Specific, Measurable, Achievable, Realistic, and Time-bound. It helps you set well-defined and realistic objectives with clear metrics and deadlines.)

Specific goals outline precisely what you want to achieve, while measurable goals allow you to track your progress. Ensure that your goals are attainable and relevant to your internship journey, considering both your abilities and the resources available to you. Lastly, set a timeframe for each goal to create a sense of urgency and structure.

Another crucial aspect of goal setting is regular evaluation. Throughout your internship, periodically review your goals and assess your progress. If necessary, adjust or add new goals to stay on track and challenge yourself. Remember, goals are not set in stone and can evolve as you gain new experiences and insights.

Finally, don't forget to celebrate your achievements along the way. Recognize and reward yourself for reaching milestones or accomplishing goals. This positive reinforcement will motivate you to keep pushing forward and make the most of your internship journey.

In summary, setting goals for your internship journey is a vital step towards achieving professional success. By reflecting on your aspirations, identifying specific areas of focus, and adopting the SMART approach, you can create meaningful and achievable goals. Regular evaluation and celebration of achievements will help you stay on track and remain motivated throughout your internship. So, embrace this opportunity and let setting goals guide you towards a fulfilling and impactful internship experience.

While I strongly advocate for a good internship program, which can be conducted both in-person and remotely, I cannot ignore the fact that there are several shortcomings in our current internship program. We aspire to create a beneficial internship program and follow the path of a successful corporate, but we must also face the reality. When we mentally prepare ourselves for this journey, the question arises: do we truly receive the value we desire from such a program? I have a distinct perspective on this matter, which I want to share with all of you in this book.

We are in need of a highly creative and innovative internship program. So far, we have been following the traditional way of conducting internships, but it is time to bring about a change. We must alter the methods and practices associated with internships and adopt new approaches. By doing so, we can create a new and practical method that caters to everyone's needs and is grounded in reality.

Chapter 3
Navigating the Summer Internship Landscape

Addressing Common Concerns and Misconceptions

This is an essential part of the internship journey, as it focuses on addressing uncertainties and clearing up misunderstandings that students commonly face when thinking about internships. In this section, our goal is to offer useful insights and practical guidance to assist students in making informed choices regarding their decision to pursue internships.

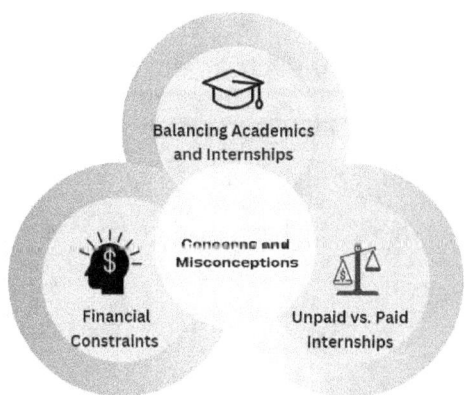

When it comes to starting an internship, many of us rely on the experiences and opinions of others around us, such as college seniors, friends, and academic coaches. However, it's essential to understand that everyone's internship experience is unique and depends on various factors like their situation, environment, industry, specialization and location. These experiences then become their perceptions about internships, which they share with you.

Sometimes, you might receive valuable advice from those who had a positive experience, but if you happen to be surrounded by people who had negative experiences, they may unintentionally exaggerate their struggles and misguide you. This can lead to a lot of confusion and make your internship journey appear daunting and uncertain.

This lack of awareness about the right approach to internships and how to handle them is a concern for me. It's common to feel overwhelmed and unsure about where to start. That's precisely why I decided to create this chapter. Drawing from my knowledge and experience, I wanted to share insights and guidance with you so that you can avoid making the same mistakes I or others may have made during our time or even in today's context.

By providing you with practical tips and a better understanding of the internship concept, I hope to equip you with the right knowledge and confidence to embark on your internship journey smoothly and make the most out of this valuable learning experience.

In the previous chapters, we addressed some common misconceptions regarding different types of internships, such as summer, remote, and international internships. Hopefully, those discussions helped to clarify any doubts you may have had.

Now, let's dive into some more fundamental aspects that will assist you in approaching your internship with a balanced and focused mindset. Our aim is to define clear goals for your internship and achieve them without any distractions. I want to emphasize that no matter what challenges you encounter, there is always a solution, but it often requires the right guidance.

By understanding the importance of setting specific objectives for your internship and seeking the right support, you can make the most of this valuable opportunity. Throughout this chapter, I'll be providing you with practical insights and advice to help you navigate your internship journey effectively and ensure a successful experience. So, let's get ready to overcome any obstacles and make the most out of your internship!

In our previous discussions, we explored various misconceptions and challenges that can arise during internships. Now, it's time to face another aspect of this journey – personal challenges that may be beyond our control. We all encounter hurdles and difficulties in life, and internships are no exception. However, instead of shying away from these problems, we should embrace them and design our approach accordingly.

Turning our problems into strengths is a powerful mindset that can help us overcome obstacles and stay focused on our goals. It's essential to acknowledge the things we can't control and find ways to adapt and navigate through them. By doing so, we can turn challenges into opportunities for growth and learning. Let's explore these misconceptions further and find the best ways to excel in our internship endeavours.

Balancing Academics and Internships:

One common concern among students is the challenge of balancing academic commitments with internship responsibilities. The fear of jeopardizing academic performance may deter some from exploring internship opportunities. However, it is essential to recognize that internships can be tailored to accommodate academic schedules. By planning ahead and setting clear expectations with internship providers and academic advisors, students can find a harmonious balance between their coursework and internship responsibilities. Flexibility and effective time management become crucial tools in navigating this challenge, allowing students to gain practical experience without compromising their academic progress.

Dealing with Financial Constraints:

Financial constraints often emerge as a legitimate concern for students considering internships, particularly if the positions are unpaid or offer low stipends. The fear of financial strain can lead some students to forego valuable internship opportunities. However, there are various solutions to address these challenges. Some internships may offer scholarships or financial assistance to support interns during their tenure. Additionally, students can explore part-time job opportunities that align with their academic schedule and internship commitments. It's also crucial to engage in open discussions with internship providers or university career services to seek advice and potential solutions for overcoming financial barriers.

Unpaid vs. Paid Internships: Weighing the Pros and Cons:

The choice between unpaid and paid internships is a topic that often sparks debates among students and academic circles. Unpaid internships may provide invaluable learning experiences, hands-on exposure to industries, and opportunities to build a professional network. However, they may present financial challenges for students who need to support themselves financially. On the other hand, paid internships offer financial compensation, which can ease the burden of expenses during the internship period. However, the learning experiences and networking opportunities in paid internships may vary compared to unpaid ones. It is essential for students to weigh the pros and cons of each type of internship and consider their personal circumstances and career goals when making this decision.

Unpaid Internships:

Pros:

1. **Valuable Learning Experience**: Unpaid internships often offer hands-on learning opportunities, allowing students to gain practical experience and apply their academic knowledge in real-world settings.

2. **Networking Opportunities:** Interns can build professional networks and connect with experienced mentors, potentially leading to future job opportunities and career growth.

3. **Flexibility:** Some unpaid internships may offer flexible working hours, allowing students to balance their academic commitments and internship responsibilities.

Cons:

1. **Financial Challenges:** Lack of compensation can be a significant drawback, as students may face financial hardships when covering living expenses during the internship period.

2. **Limited Accessibility:** Unpaid internships may not be feasible for students with financial obligations or those who need to support themselves financially.

3. **Perception of Exploitation:** Some unpaid internships have faced criticism for potentially exploiting students' efforts without providing fair compensation.

Paid Internships:

Pros:

1. **Financial Support:** Paid internships offer monetary compensation, helping students cover their living expenses and reduce financial burdens.

2. **Enhanced Motivation:** Monetary rewards can serve as an added incentive, encouraging interns to perform at their best and take their roles seriously.

3. **Value Recognition:** Paid internships may signal that the organization values the intern's contribution and expertise, leading to a more fulfilling experience.

Cons:

1. **Competition:** Paid internships tend to be more competitive, making it challenging for students to secure these positions.

2. **Possible Focus on Menial Tasks:** Some paid internships may prioritize cost-effectiveness, leading to interns being assigned to repetitive or less impactful tasks.

3. **Limited Learning Opportunities:** In some cases, paid interns might have less exposure to senior-level

professionals or decision-making processes compared to their unpaid counterparts.

Ultimately, the decision between unpaid and paid internships will depend on individual circumstances, financial constraints, and career goals. Both types of internships can offer valuable experiences and contribute to a student's professional development. Students should carefully consider the pros and cons of each option before making their choice.

While discussing the various types of internships, we also delved into the pros and cons of paid and unpaid internships. However, there exists a different world of internships where you receive compensation for your work, but the experience is altogether different from best experience.

I want to emphasize that as we talk about effective approaches, it's important to acknowledge certain difficult truths that might be present in certain organizations. It's important to approach this topic with a balanced perspective and be prepared for potential challenges that could arise in the real-world scenarios. When you opt for a paid internship, some companies may treat you as a mere resource without much concern for your purpose or growth. They might believe that an intern, earning a stipend, can accomplish more work than a permanent employee.

Many organizations prefer temporary hires, especially for short-term projects lasting a few months, where they intend to complete their work without investing in hiring permanent employee. It is crucial to be cautious of such paid internship's practices, where the objective is not to nurture your development as an intern, but rather to get their short-term projects done with minimal expenditure.

Allow me to share a real-time example from the IT industry, particularly in digital marketing. Some organizations seek interns to run social campaigns for 2 to 3 months. They provide only a week of training, and then interns are left to manage the campaigns in the name of a digital marketing internship. While they may pay you a stipend, the learning and experience in such scenarios are often limited, and the focus is on the company's objectives rather than your personal growth.

Let me illustrate this theory further with same example. Imagine a large real estate corporation that launches new projects annually. They want to target a specific middle-class family demographic through a social media campaign on Facebook. Instead of using their existing employees, they prefer to hire interns, train them on how to run the Facebook campaign, track its progress, and generate leads. These leads are then transferred to the sales department for every project launch.

The campaign cycle is relatively short, typically lasting 2 to 3 months per project. The interns are tasked with managing the campaign during this period. I've observed that companies often provide minimal guidance to interns and expect them to run the campaign without much context of long-term objectives. This leads to a situation where interns are merely learning how to operate a campaign on Facebook, but they may not be solving any real business problems.

If you're considering this internship, ask yourself whether you genuinely care about solving business problems. If you aim to gain a deeper understanding of the real world and use this experience to secure a meaningful job, then this internship may not be the best fit. Keep in mind that companies are focused on their own objectives, and as long as you're getting paid, they may not prioritize your learning and development.

When you're in the job market and interviewing for a digital marketing role, employers may ask how you stand out from other candidates and what you've learned during your internship. If you're unable to answer these questions convincingly, it could be because you didn't have the opportunity to participate in crucial discussions or understand the project's strategic aspects.

To truly add value during your internship, you need to know what course corrections are needed when your campaign isn't yielding good outcomes. Analyze your campaign, refine it, and target a new audience if necessary. This requires collaboration with the sales and marketing teams of the real estate company to understand their challenges and business objectives.

Keep in mind that running a Facebook campaign isn't just a typical intern project; it has real implications for the company's success in the real estate market. The speed at which their properties are sold depends on various marketing efforts, including physical campaigns and email marketing. To succeed, you must be diligent and thoughtful in your approach, and you cannot work in isolation. I hope this clarifies the point.

I don't mean to say that you won't learn anything during a 3-month paid internship; surely, there will be some learning. However, the value it adds to your career aspirations and future job prospects may not be as significant. It's essential to be aware of such short-term gains that might not contribute much to your long-term career goals.

Identifying Summer Internship Opportunities

In the initial stages, many students feel disheartened because there's a misconception that internships come easily if you have a strong network. While this can be true sometimes, it's not always the case. That's why it's important to understand that finding a good internship, whether local or international, requires the same level of dedication and hard work. The more you put into it, the higher your chances of succeeding and securing an excellent internship.

As the saying goes, "Where there is a will, there is a way." This holds true for internships as well. So, give your best effort and don't settle for less. Remember, you're at the initial stage of your internship journey, and it's not a point where failure defines you. You have a long road ahead to achieve your goals. Stay consistent, work hard, and don't compromise on your efforts. Your determination will pay off in the end.

Securing a summer internship is a crucial step in your journey towards professional success. Not only does it provide you with valuable hands-on experience, but it also offers an opportunity to network with industry professionals and explore potential career paths.

However, finding the right internship can be a discouraging task, especially when faced with numerous options and fierce competition. In this subchapter, we will guide you through the process of identifying summer internship opportunities that align with your goals and aspirations.

IDENTIFY A RIGHT OPPORTUNITY

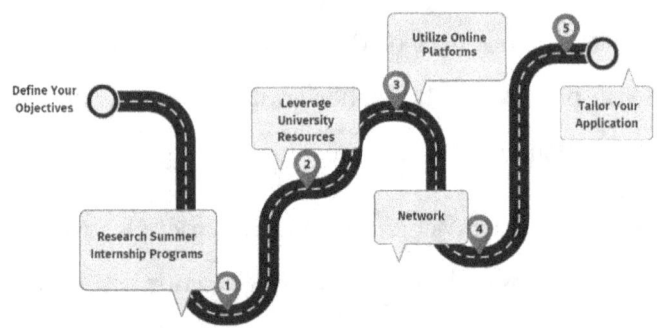

1. **Define Your Objectives:** Start by determining what you hope to gain from your summer internship experience. Are you looking to gain industry-specific skills, explore a particular career field, or expand your professional network? Clearly defining your objectives will help you narrow down your search and focus on opportunities that align with your goals.

2. **Research Summer Internship Programs:** Begin your search by researching various summer internship programs. Look

into organizations, companies, and institutions that offer internships in your desired field or industry. Consider both local and international opportunities, as they can provide unique experiences and broaden your horizons.

3. **Leverage University Resources:** Many universities have dedicated career centres or internship offices that can assist you in finding summer internships. They often have established relationships with companies and can provide valuable guidance and resources. Attend career fairs, workshops, and networking events organized by your university to connect with potential internship providers.

4. **Utilize Online Platforms:** Numerous online platforms specialize in connecting students with internship opportunities. Online portals and websites can help you discover a wide range of internships, including remote positions. Create a compelling online profile, upload your resume, and actively search for internships that match your interests and qualifications.

5. **Network:** Networking is a powerful tool when it comes to finding internships. Reach out to professionals in your desired field, attend industry conferences, and join relevant professional associations. Building meaningful connections

can lead to internship opportunities that may not be advertised publicly.

6. **Tailor Your Application Materials**: When applying for summer internships, it is essential to tailor your resume, cover letter, and portfolio to each opportunity. Highlight relevant skills, experiences, and academic achievements that align with the internship requirements. Additionally, proofread your application materials thoroughly to ensure they are error-free and professional.

Remember, securing a summer internship requires effort, persistence, and a proactive approach. Be open to different opportunities, even if they are not your first choice, as each internship experience can provide valuable insights and help shape your career path. Stay organized, stay focused, and stay motivated - your dream summer internship is within reach!

Researching and Applying for Summer Internships

Just as you research before buying a house or making any big decision, it's also important to research before taking an internship. Just like you wouldn't buy a house without knowing about it.

Still not convinced?

When you're considering purchasing a laptop, desktop, or even a mobile phone, you put in a lot of effort to research. You look into the specifications, the model, apps marketplace, and how it looks and feels. The goal is to ensure that what you're buying meets your needs because you don't want to make a mistake. After all, buying these things requires your hard-earned money, and you don't want to risk spending money again in just a few months. Isn't that, right?

That's why you're careful and thorough in your research before investing in your favourite gadgets. So, why not apply the same level of determination and logic when researching internships? Just like you wouldn't want to waste your money on something that doesn't suit you, you also wouldn't want to waste your time on an internship that doesn't align with your goals. Your future is just as important as your investments, so it makes sense to do your best in finding the right opportunity.

As a student or trainee, the summer break presents a valuable opportunity to gain hands-on experience and enhance your professional skills through internships. Whether you are interested in an internship locally or internationally, or even considering a remote internship, this subchapter will provide you with a comprehensive guide on how to research and apply for summer internships.

Researching potential internships is a crucial first step in finding the right opportunity that aligns with your career goals and interests. Start by identifying the industries or fields you are passionate about and want to explore further. Consider reaching out to your professors, academic advisors, or career services office for recommendations or resources related to internships in your desired niche.

Utilize online platforms and job boards specifically tailored for internships. These platforms often provide a wide range of opportunities and allow you to filter based on location, industry, or duration. Additionally, consider joining industry-specific forums or professional networking groups to connect with professionals who can offer insights or potential internship leads.

When conducting your research, keep an open mind and consider both paid and unpaid internships. While paid internships may be more competitive, they often provide financial support and valuable experience. On the other hand, unpaid internships can still offer significant learning opportunities and help you build a strong network within your chosen field.

Once you have identified potential internships, it is time to tailor your application materials to highlight your skills and experiences relevant to each opportunity. Craft a compelling resume and cover letter that demonstrate your passion, commitment, and eagerness to learn. Be sure to customize each application to reflect the specific requirements and objectives of the internship you are applying for.

Prepare for interviews by researching the organization, its values, and recent projects or initiatives. Practice common interview questions and think of examples from your past experiences that illustrate your strengths and problem-solving abilities. Additionally, be prepared to discuss your career goals and how the internship aligns with your long-term plans.

Remember to follow up with a thank-you note or email after each interview to express your gratitude and reiterate your interest in the internship. This thoughtful gesture can leave a lasting impression on the hiring manager.

In summary, researching and applying for summer internships requires proactive effort and careful preparation. By conducting thorough research, tailoring your application materials, and preparing for interviews, you will significantly increase your chances of securing a summer internship that will enhance your professional development and pave the way for future success.

While pursuing internships, every student experiences their own unique journey. Some may have exceptionally positive experiences, while others might encounter challenges along the way. When preparing for an internship, it's crucial to follow some best practices that can serve as a helpful guide. These practices act as a mirror, reflecting the situation and providing valuable insights. By doing so, you can increase your chances of finding a well-suited and rewarding internship. However, in the real world, there could be many best practices to explore, and each individual's experience may vary. The key is to remain open-minded, persistent, and adaptable as you navigate the internship journey, learning and growing from each opportunity that comes your way.

I have gathered a collection of best practices that I've come across, either from my experiences in the industry or through insights shared by my friends and colleagues who directly managed interns in their organizations. These practices serve as valuable lessons for those involved in the internship journey.

While I acknowledge that these practices might not encompass all the best approaches, they offer significant guidance and insights to enhance the internship experience. As students, incorporating these practices can contribute to a more rewarding and enriching internship journey. Remember that the internship landscape is diverse and ever-evolving, so staying receptive to new ideas and experiences can lead to continuous growth and success in the professional world.

Best Practices for Students Applying for Internships

For some college graduates, finding a great internship is made easier with the support and guidance they receive from their family, friends, or college/university. However, there are many others who lack proper guidance in this process. That's why I've compiled a list of best practices for applying to internships in any organization. It may not cover everything, but I hope it provides you with the right guidance. I hope you find something valuable in it!

Research and Target: Make sure to do comprehensive research on companies and industries that match your career interests. Get a good grasp of their business model, focusing on your area of interest. After that, aim for internships that align with your skills, aspirations, and values.

Tailor Your Resume and Cover Letter: It's a good practice to customize your resume each time you apply. Since every organization is different, it's important to adjust your resume accordingly. Make sure to personalize your resume and cover letter for each internship application. Highlight your relevant experiences, skills, and achievements that match the specific opportunity.

Leverage Your Network: Utilize your professional network, including professors, career advisors, and alumni, to seek advice, recommendations, and potential internship opportunities.

Prepare for Interviews: Practice common interview questions and be ready to discuss your experiences, strengths, and career goals confidently during interviews.

Showcase Your Skills: Create a portfolio or online presence (e.g., LinkedIn profile, personal website) to showcase your projects, achievements, and skills to prospective employers.

Follow Application Instructions: Pay close attention to internship application requirements and deadlines. Submit all requested documents and information promptly and accurately.

Demonstrate Enthusiasm and Initiative: Show genuine enthusiasm for the internship and the company. Demonstrate initiative by asking thoughtful questions and expressing interest in contributing to the organization.

Professional Communication: Maintain professional communication throughout the application process. Respond promptly to emails and follow-up messages in a polite and courteous manner.

Be Persistent and Patient: Understand that the internship search process can be competitive and time-consuming. Be persistent in your efforts and remain patient as you wait for responses.

Stay Open-Minded: Consider both paid and unpaid internships and be open to exploring opportunities in different industries or locations. Each experience can provide valuable insights and skill development.

Seek Feedback: If you receive a rejection, don't be discouraged. Request feedback from interviewers or mentors to identify areas for improvement and apply it to future applications.

Reflect and Learn: After each application or interview, take time to reflect on the experience. Identify what went well and areas for growth, continuously improving your approach.

By following these best practices, you can enhance your internship application process and increase your chances of securing meaningful and rewarding internship opportunities. Remember, internships serve as essential stepping stones in your professional journey, allowing you to gain valuable experiences and grow both personally and professionally.

Crafting an Impressive Resume and Cover Letter

Your resume is not just a academic or personal story; it's your professional story as well. It's crucial to master the art of storytelling when crafting your resume.

In today's competitive world, a well-crafted resume and cover letter are essential tools that can help you stand out from the crowd. Whether you are searching for an internship, summer internship, international internship, or remote internship, these documents play a crucial role in making a strong first impression on potential employers. This subchapter will guide students and interns through the process of creating an impressive resume and cover letter that will pave the way to professional success.

The first step in crafting an impressive resume is to understand its purpose. A resume serves as a snapshot of your skills, experiences, and qualifications. It should be concise, organized, and tailored to the specific internship position you are applying for. This subchapter will provide guidance on how to structure your resume effectively, highlighting your relevant experience and showcasing your accomplishments.

Additionally, we will delve into the art of writing a compelling cover letter. A cover letter allows you to introduce yourself to potential employers, explain why you are interested in the internship, and demonstrate how your skills align with the organization's goals. We will explore the key elements that should be included in a cover letter, such as a strong opening statement, relevant experiences, and a closing paragraph that expresses your enthusiasm for the opportunity.

Moreover, this subchapter will provide tips and strategies to make your resume and cover letter stand out. From choosing the right font and format to utilizing action verbs and keywords, we will explore various techniques that can make your application materials visually appealing and impactful. We will also discuss the importance of proofreading and seeking feedback from mentors or career advisors to ensure that your resume and cover letter are error-free and convey your unique strengths effectively.

Lastly, we recognize that internships come in different forms, including summer internships, international internships, and remote internships. We will address how to tailor your resume and cover letter to each specific type of internship, highlighting the skills and experiences that are most relevant to these opportunities.

By following the guidance provided in this subchapter, students and interns will gain the knowledge and tools necessary to craft impressive resumes and cover letters that will captivate potential employers and increase their chances of securing their desired internships. Remember, your resume and cover letter are your first steps towards professional success.

Tips and Techniques for Resume and Cover Letter

Applying tips and techniques in their resume and cover letter is crucial for students because it enhances their chances of making a strong and positive impression on potential employers. The resume is often the first document employers see, and a well-crafted one can quickly capture their attention. By highlighting relevant experiences, quantifying achievements, and using action verbs, students can showcase their skills and accomplishments effectively, making them stand out among other applicants.

A customized and targeted resume and cover letter demonstrate a student's genuine interest in the internship or company. Employers appreciate candidates who have taken the time to research the organization and align their application with its specific needs and values. This attention to detail indicates the student's commitment and dedication, increasing their chances of being considered for the internship.

An impressive resume and cover letter also help students showcase their transferable skills and potential contributions to the company. By clearly communicating their abilities and passion for the role, students can demonstrate how they can bring value to the organization. This not only boosts their chances of getting selected for the internship but also enhances their overall employability and professional brand.

Additionally, having a resume and cover letter that are written well and free of mistakes shows that you take your job application seriously and pay attention to the little things. Employers may not consider applications with spelling or grammar mistakes as it suggests a lack of effort. On the flip side, a polished application indicates that you're dependable and possess strong communication abilities, qualities that are highly esteemed in the professional realm.

Research the Company: Before crafting your resume and cover letter, thoroughly research the company you're applying to. Understand their values, culture, and industry focus to tailor your application to their specific needs.

Highlight Relevant Experience: Emphasize relevant academic projects, extracurricular activities, and part-time jobs that demonstrate your skills and align with the internship position.

Use Action Verbs: Start bullet points with strong action verbs to showcase your achievements and contributions effectively, such as "developed," "implemented," or "collaborated."

Quantify Accomplishments: Wherever possible, include measurable outcomes and results to demonstrate your impact and effectiveness in previous roles.

Customize for Each Application: Tailor both your resume and cover letter for each internship application, addressing the specific requirements mentioned in the job posting.

Showcase Transferable Skills: Highlight transferable skills like communication, problem-solving, and teamwork, which are valuable across various industries.

Be Concise and Clear: Keep your resume and cover letter concise and easy to read. Avoid long paragraphs and use bullet points to present information effectively.

Professional Formatting: Use a clean and professional format for both your resume and cover letter. Choose an appropriate font and ensure consistency in formatting.

Proofread Carefully: Double-check for any spelling or grammatical errors in your application materials. Typos can create a negative impression on potential employers.

Include a Strong Opening: Start your cover letter with a compelling introduction that grabs the reader's attention and showcases your enthusiasm for the internship.

Address the Hiring Manager: If possible, address your cover letter to the hiring manager or the relevant person within the company.

Showcase Your Knowledge: Demonstrate your knowledge about the company and express your passion for working with them in your cover letter.

Be Professional and Polite: Maintain a professional tone throughout your resume and cover letter. Use polite language and thank the reader for considering your application.

Provide Contact Information: Include updated contact information, such as your email address and phone number, so that the company can easily reach you.

Seek Feedback: Before submitting your application, seek feedback from mentors, career advisors, or peers to ensure your materials are compelling and error-free.

By following these techniques, you can create an impressive resume and cover letter that showcases your skills, passion, and suitability for the internship position. A well-crafted application can significantly increase your chances of standing out and landing your desired internship in the corporate world.

"First impressions are lasting impressions."

Preparing for Summer Internship Interviews

Securing a summer internship is a crucial step in building a successful career. Not only do internships provide valuable hands-on experience, but they also open doors to potential job offers and help you develop a professional network. However, before embarking on your internship journey, it is essential to prepare for the interview process. This subchapter will provide you with valuable tips and strategies to excel in your summer internship interviews.

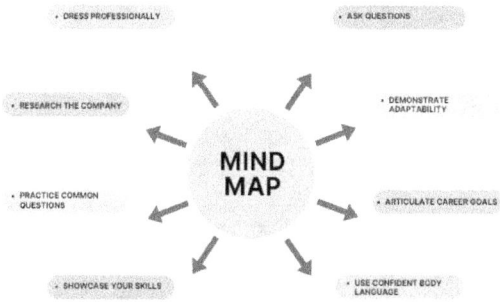

Research and Preparation

First and foremost, research the company or organization you are interviewing with. Familiarize yourself with their mission, values, and recent projects. Understanding their goals and objectives will enable you to tailor your answers during the interview and demonstrate your genuine interest in their work.

Next, analyze the internship position you have applied for. Review the job description in detail and identify the skills, qualifications, and experiences they are seeking. This will allow you to align your own experiences and highlight relevant accomplishments during the interview.

Highlighting Your Skills and Experiences

During the interview, be prepared to discuss your skills and experiences that make you a strong candidate for the internship. Reflect on your past experiences, such as academic projects, part-time jobs, or volunteering, and identify the transferable skills you have gained.

Additionally, showcase your ability to work in a team and your problem-solving skills. Interviewers often look for candidates who can collaborate effectively and think critically. Provide concrete examples of situations where you successfully resolved a problem or worked collaboratively to achieve a goal.

Behavioural and Situational Questions

Internship interviews often include behavioural and situational questions to assess your ability to handle real-life scenarios. Prepare for these questions by reflecting on past experiences and considering how you would respond to different situations. Practice answering questions that highlight your ability to adapt, communicate, and work under pressure.

Professionalism and Communication

Finally, remember to present yourself professionally during the interview. Dress appropriately, maintain good posture, and make eye contact. Practice active listening and engage in the conversation by asking thoughtful questions about the internship program or company culture.

Preparing for summer internship interviews is crucial to increase your chances of securing a valuable internship opportunity. By conducting thorough research, highlighting relevant skills and experiences, and practicing your interview skills, you will be well-equipped to impress potential employers. Remember, the interview is an opportunity for you to showcase your talents and potential, so make the most out of it.

Making the Most of Your Summer Internship Experience

As a student or trainee, embarking on an internship can be an exciting and crucial step towards your future professional success. Whether you are pursuing an internship during the summer or considering international or remote internships, it is important to make the most of this valuable experience. This subchapter will guide you on how to maximize your summer internship experience, regardless of the type of internship you choose.

First and foremost, it is essential to approach your internship with a positive mindset and a willingness to learn. Remember that internships are designed to provide you with practical exposure and real-world skills. Be proactive in seeking out new opportunities, taking on challenging tasks, and asking for feedback. By demonstrating your enthusiasm and dedication, you will leave a lasting impression on your supervisors and colleagues.

Networking is another crucial aspect of making the most of your internship experience. Take advantage of the opportunity to build professional relationships and expand your network. Attend company events, engage in conversations with professionals in your field, and connect with fellow interns. These connections can be invaluable for future job opportunities and mentorship.

Additionally, make it a priority to set clear goals and objectives for your internship. What specific skills or knowledge do you hope to gain? Are there any particular projects or tasks you want to be involved in? By having a clear vision, you can communicate your goals to your supervisor and work towards achieving them throughout the internship.

Besides, do not underestimate the power of reflection and self-evaluation. Regularly assess your progress, strengths, and areas for improvement. Take the time to write in a journal or discuss your experiences with a mentor. This self-reflection will enable you to identify your personal and professional growth and make adjustments as needed.

Lastly, embrace the diverse opportunities that summer internships, international internships, or remote internships can offer. Emphasize the importance of cultural sensitivity, adaptability, and open-mindedness. Working in different environments and with people from various backgrounds will enhance your interpersonal skills and broaden your perspective.

Your summer internship experience holds immense potential for your professional development. By maintaining a positive attitude, actively networking, setting clear goals, reflecting on your progress, and embracing diverse opportunities, you can ensure that your internship becomes a stepping stone towards a successful career.

Chapter 4

Exploring International Internship Opportunities

Understanding the Benefits of International Internships

In today's tough job market, having real-world work experience is crucial for students and interns to distinguish themselves. Internships are a wonderful chance to build skills, discover various career options, and establish priceless connections. And in the context of internships, international opportunities can offer an unmatched edge.

You might be considering that securing a local internship is already quite a significant task, and now the author wishes to discuss international internships. One might question the rationale behind even contemplating an international internship. Could it be perceived as an ambitious and impractical dream? Rest assured, fellow explorers, as the situation has evolved, and we can attribute (or assign responsibility) to a variety of factors for this transformation. In an era of heightened global interconnectivity, organizations are actively seeking diverse talents across geographical boundaries. International internships now offer a unique chance to collaborate with individuals from diverse cultural backgrounds, enriching your global outlook.

International internships are not as elusive as they once seemed. People are applying smartly, and guess what? They are actually landing those opportunities! It's all about showcasing your skills, talents, and creativity - be a unicorn in a world of regular horses, and companies will come running!

So, let's change the narrative, shall we? International internships are no longer on some faraway cloud. They're within your grasp! Get ready to conquer the global stage with your unique abilities. The world is waiting for your awesomeness!

If you're not ready to believe it now, that's alright, but international internships are already happening all around us, and their prevalence will only increase with time. Examples of successful international internships will continue to grow, and in a few years, you might witness how these boundaries that seem like limitations today will no longer hold us back. The world is becoming more interconnected, and opportunities are expanding beyond borders.

International internships go beyond the traditional boundaries of a local internship, offering students the chance to immerse themselves in a different culture, language, and work environment. This subchapter aims to shed light on the numerous benefits that international internships can bring to students and interns, whether they are looking to pursue a career in business, engineering, or any other field.

First and foremost, international internships provide a unique chance to expand one's horizons and gain a global perspective. Working in a different country exposes interns to diverse cultures, customs, and ways of doing business. This exposure helps develop adaptability, cross-cultural communication skills, and a global mindset, all of which are highly valued traits in today's interconnected world.

Moreover, international internships offer an incredible opportunity to network on an international scale. By working alongside professionals from different countries, interns can build a global network of contacts, potentially opening doors to future job opportunities in various parts of the world. These connections can also lead to mentorship opportunities, where experienced professionals can provide guidance and insights into the global industry.

Additionally, international internships allow students to enhance their language skills. Immersion in a foreign work environment provides an excellent chance to practice and improve language proficiency, which can be a valuable asset in today's globalized job market. Being able to communicate effectively in multiple languages can greatly increase one's career prospects and open up doors to international job opportunities.

Another benefit of international internships is the exposure to different work practices and methodologies. Each country has its unique approaches to business, and by experiencing diverse work cultures, interns can gain a broader skill set and a more comprehensive understanding of their chosen field. This exposure to different work environments can also foster creativity and innovation, as interns learn to think outside the box and adapt to new challenges.

International internships offer a wide range of benefits to students and interns. From gaining a global perspective and expanding professional networks to improving language skills and developing adaptability, the advantages are numerous. By embracing international internships, students and interns can pave their path to professional success and gain a competitive edge in today's global job market. Whether it is a summer internship, remote internship, or any other type, exploring international opportunities is a step towards personal and professional growth.

Researching and Applying for International Internships

This is a crucial aspect to consider because if you lack knowledge about applying for international internships, then you might struggle with managing the internship itself. Therefore, it's vital to pay close attention to this chapter, especially if you have aspirations of pursuing an internship on an international level. Whether it's in-person or remote, an international internship refers to working with a company located outside your own country, in a foreign land. So, get ready to broaden your horizons and explore exciting opportunities worldwide!

Researching and applying for international internships can be an exciting and rewarding experience for students. Whether you are seeking an internship during the summer or looking for a remote internship opportunity, this subchapter will provide you with valuable guidance on how to navigate the process and maximize your chances of success.

To begin with, researching international internships requires careful planning and an understanding of your goals and interests. Start by identifying the countries or regions where you would like to gain experience. Consider factors such as language requirements, cultural differences, and the industries prevalent in those locations. This step will help you narrow down your search and focus on internships that align with your career aspirations.

Once you have identified your desired locations, it is crucial to conduct thorough research on the internships available. Utilize online platforms, internship databases, and professional networks to find opportunities that match your interests. Additionally, reach out to your university's career services office or internship coordinators who may have information on international internship programs. They can provide guidance and valuable resources to aid your search.

Research plays a crucial role in applying for an international internship. You should break down your research into smaller, logical pieces and align them with your skills and capabilities. For instance, if you wish to apply for an internship in the logistics department of an organization because you are pursuing a master's degree with a specialization in supply chain management, it's important to gain a thorough understanding of the logistics department, despite not having prior experience in this specific business function.

Now, why would a company consider you for this internship just because you have supply chain management as your specialization? Here's the trick: you need to comprehend the value chain and ecosystem of the organization. Suppose the company is a manufacturing organization, whether it deals with processes, automotive, or industrial products. In that case, you should conduct a deep dive into the specific sector the company operates in, such as the automotive industry.

By doing so, you'll understand the products they sell in the market and identify the supply chain requirements. Thorough research is necessary to comprehend the value stream of the supply chain. Additionally, studying their competitors will provide a fresh perspective and allow for meaningful comparisons.

You should explore various approaches to understand the supply chain. Conduct market research to identify the typical challenges in the industry and those specific to the company's supply chain. Utilize resources like Google, websites, customer research, and financial reports to pinpoint the problems companies are facing.

Having understood the value chain and logistics operations of the company, along with the major business problems, you can craft a concise and intelligent summary. When applying for an internship, ensure you share this unique perspective with the company. Express your genuine interest and seriousness in contributing to solving their problems. Also, share your project ideas and when you'd like to undertake the internship.

Believe me, they will be thrilled to find someone outside their organization showing such enthusiasm and a deep understanding of their challenges. Whether you can solve all their problems or not may not be the point, but your passion and excitement will make a lasting impression, opening doors to the right opportunities in the right company.

When applying for international internships, it is essential to tailor your application materials to each organization. Update your resume, highlighting relevant skills, experiences, and coursework. Craft a compelling cover letter that showcases your motivation, international perspective, and desire to learn. Be sure to mention any language proficiency or cross-cultural experiences that may set you apart from other candidates. Don't forget to add your point of view of their problem statement or challenges.

Let's discuss some essential hygiene and operational activities that you need to manage while applying for an international internship. It's crucial to take care of these logistical aspects alongside the application process. Consider factors such as visa requirements, travel arrangements, and other necessary preparations. By addressing these aspects efficiently, you can have a smoother and well-organized experience during your international internship journey.

Research the visa requirements, duration of stay, and financial implications associated with living abroad. It is important to have a clear understanding of the costs involved and explore potential funding options such as scholarships or grants.

Lastly, be proactive in your application process by reaching out to potential supervisors or organizations directly. Networking can play a significant role in securing an international internship. Attend career fairs, industry conferences, or virtual events where you can connect with professionals in your field of interest.

In summary, researching and applying for international internships requires careful planning, thorough research, and proactive networking. By following these guidelines, you will increase your chances of securing a valuable internship experience that aligns with your career goals. Whether it is a summer internship, a remote opportunity, or an international placement, this subchapter provides you with the necessary tools to navigate the path to professional success.

With that being said, let's maintain an optimistic and positive outlook that the visa situation will improve over time, and companies will offer suitable positions. Now, let's shift our attention back to the topic of applying for international internships.

Let's have a reality check here. Researching foreign summer internships and local internships both demand a similar level of effort, but pursuing an international internship involves some additional considerations. Before applying for an international internship, there are many factors to think about. While you need to ensure that you're eligible to work in that country, understand its geopolitical situation, overall stability, and economic condition. These aspects might not be as important when seeking an internship within your own country, but they become crucial when considering international opportunities.

Before diving into researching, applying, and convincing an organization for an international internship, it's essential to be sure that the execution is feasible. You wouldn't want to put in all that effort only to realize later that certain factors make the internship impractical, as I mentioned before. This is why I'm emphasizing the importance of considering the steps involved and doing your research about the country as well.

For instance, imagine you're passionate about studying natural gas and sustainability as part of your internship in energy program. While Afghanistan might be a beautiful country, the political instability there might not favour your plans for a safe and productive internship experience. It's crucial to consider all these aspects before you fully commit. I believe this example provides you with straightforward and factual instances that help clarify my points effectively.

Preparing for International Internship Interviews

Interviews are an essential part of the application process for international internships. To increase your chances of success, it is crucial to prepare thoroughly and showcase your skills and qualifications effectively. This subchapter will guide you through the necessary steps to prepare for international internship interviews, ensuring that you are well-equipped to impress potential employers.

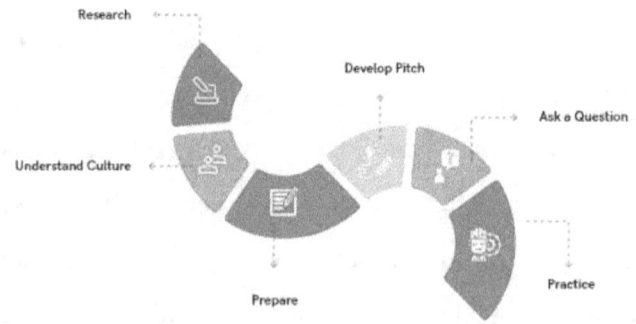

Research the Company and Internship Opportunity:

Before attending any interview, it is important to research the company and the specific internship opportunity you are applying for. Familiarize yourself with the company's mission, values, and recent projects. Understand the scope of the internship and how it aligns with your career goals. This will allow you to tailor your answers during the interview and demonstrate your genuine interest in the organization.

1. **Understand Cultural Differences**: If you are applying for an international internship, it is essential to be aware of cultural differences that may affect the interview process. Research the country's business customs, etiquette, and communication styles. Being aware of these cultural nuances will help you adapt your approach, ensuring you make a positive impression on the interviewer.

2. **Prepare Common Interview Questions:** Practice common interview questions to refine your responses and boost your confidence. Questions may include, "Tell us about yourself," "Why are you interested in this internship?" and "What skills do you bring to the table?" Craft concise, well-thought-out answers that highlight your strengths, achievements, and how they relate to the internship opportunity.

3. **Develop a Strong Elevator Pitch:** An elevator pitch is a brief, compelling summary of your skills, experience, and career goals. Craft an elevator pitch that showcases your unique qualities and demonstrates why you are the ideal candidate for the internship. This concise introduction should leave a lasting impression on the interviewer.

4. **Prepare Questions to Ask:** Prepare thoughtful questions to ask the interviewer. This not only shows your genuine interest in the internship but also helps you assess whether the opportunity is the right fit for you. Inquire about the company culture, potential projects, and the intern's role within the organization. Remember, an interview is a two-way conversation, and your questions can demonstrate your enthusiasm and curiosity.

Be informed that asking questions does not mean you need to bombard the interviewer with queries. Be selective and ask questions that genuinely interest you and add value to the conversation. Thoughtful questions can leave a positive impression and enhance your chances of securing the internship opportunity.

- **Demonstrates Interest:** By asking thoughtful and relevant questions, you show genuine interest in the company and the internship opportunity. It signals to the interviewer that you have done your research and are engaged in the conversation.

- **Expands Understanding**: Asking questions provides you with a chance to gain deeper insights into the company's culture, values, and work environment. Understanding these aspects can help you assess if the organization aligns with your own career goals and preferences.

- **Clarifies Expectations**: Inquiring about the responsibilities, tasks, and projects involved in the internship allows you to understand the role better. It helps you gauge if the internship will provide the learning and experiences you seek.

- **Highlights Enthusiasm**: Engaging in a dialogue with the interviewer demonstrates enthusiasm and eagerness to learn. It shows that you are proactive and keen on making a positive impact during your internship.

- **Builds Rapport**: Asking questions can create a positive rapport with the interviewer. It fosters a two-way conversation, making the interaction more enjoyable and memorable.

- **Shows Critical Thinking:** Thoughtful questions showcase your critical thinking skills and curiosity about the company's operations and industry trends.
- **Helps in Decision-Making:** The answers to your questions can aid in making an informed decision about accepting the internship if it is offered. It allows you to evaluate whether the opportunity aligns with your personal and professional goals.
- **Leaves a Lasting Impression:** Being engaged and asking questions can leave a lasting impression on the interviewer. It differentiates you from other candidates who may not have demonstrated the same level of curiosity and initiative.

Practice with Mock Interviews: To gain confidence and refine your interview skills, practice with mock interviews. Seek feedback from mentors, professors, or career counsellors who can provide valuable insights and suggestions for improvement. Mock interviews will help you identify areas of weakness and allow you to fine-tune your answers before the actual interview.

The tips for mock interviews suggested below are based on a combination of common best practices in interview preparation and effective communication techniques. These tips draw from expert advice provided by career development professionals, interview coaches, and hiring managers. Additionally, they are aligned with commonly recommended strategies to enhance interview performance and build confidence in candidates seeking internships or job opportunities.

- **Treat it Like a Real Interview**: Approach the mock interview with the same level of seriousness and professionalism as you would a real interview. This will help you gain a more accurate assessment of your interview skills.
- **Research the Company and Role**: Familiarize yourself with the company and the position you are interviewing for. This will enable you to answer questions more confidently and tailor your responses to the specific role.
- **Practice Common Questions**: Prepare for common interview questions, such as "Tell me about yourself," "Why do you want this internship," and "What are your strengths and weaknesses?" Practice your responses to ensure clarity and conciseness.
- **Practice Non-Verbal Communication**: Pay attention to your non-verbal cues, such as eye contact, body language, and facial expressions. These elements

contribute to how you come across during the interview.

- **Manage Nervousness**: Take deep breaths and stay composed during the mock interview. Remember that it's a learning opportunity, and everyone experiences nerves.
- **Seek Feedback**: After the mock interview, ask for feedback from the interviewer. Inquire about areas of improvement and specific ways to enhance your interview performance.
- **Record the Session**: If possible, record the mock interview to review later. This can help you identify areas where you can improve your responses and delivery.
- **Practice with Different Interviewers**: Conduct mock interviews with different individuals to experience various interview styles and feedback perspectives.
- **Reflect and Learn**: After each mock interview, take time to reflect on your performance. Identify strengths and areas for improvement to focus on during future practice sessions.
- **Focus on Soft Skills:** Pay attention to how you communicate, problem-solve, and showcase your interpersonal skills during the mock interview.

- **Prepare Questions to Ask:** Have a list of thoughtful questions to ask the mock interviewer at the end of the session. This demonstrates your interest in the position and company.

Mock interviews are valuable opportunities to fine-tune your interviewing skills and gain confidence. Utilize these tips to make the most of your mock interview practice and enhance your overall interview performance.

By following these steps, you will be well-prepared to tackle international internship interviews. Remember, thorough preparation and a confident, professional demeanour will greatly increase your chances of securing the internship opportunity you desire. Good luck on your journey to professional success!

Overcoming Challenges and Adapting to a New Culture

Embarking on an internship is an exciting and transformative experience, offering students and interns the opportunity to gain valuable skills and knowledge in their chosen field. However, internships often come with their fair share of challenges, especially when it involves stepping out of your comfort zone and adapting to a new culture. Whether you are participating in a summer internship, an international internship, or a remote internship, the ability to overcome these challenges and adapt to a new environment is crucial for your professional success.

One of the first challenges you may face when interning in a new culture is the language barrier. Communication is the key to success in any workplace, and being able to effectively communicate with colleagues and supervisors is essential. Take advantage of language learning resources, such as apps, language classes, or language exchange programs, to improve your language skills. Additionally, don't hesitate to ask for clarification or help when needed and be proactive in seeking opportunities to practice your language skills.

Another challenge you may encounter is cultural differences. Every culture has its own set of norms, values, and customs. It is important to approach these differences with an open mind and a willingness to learn. Take the time to educate yourself about the cultural practices and etiquette of your host country or organization. This will not only help you navigate social situations but also foster positive relationships with your colleagues.

Adapting to a new work environment can also be challenging. Each organization has its own unique work culture and expectations. Be observant and adaptable, paying attention to how things are done and adjusting your approach accordingly.

Seek feedback from your supervisors and colleagues to ensure that you are meeting expectations and making the most of your internship experience.

Lastly, whether you are participating in a summer, international, or remote internship, homesickness can be a common challenge. Being away from familiar surroundings and loved ones can be difficult, but with the right support system, you can overcome this hurdle. Stay connected with friends and family through regular communication, explore your new surroundings, and engage in activities that bring you joy. Remember, embracing the new culture and fully immersing yourself in the experience will help alleviate homesickness.

By acknowledging and addressing these challenges head-on, you will not only overcome them but also grow both personally and professionally. An internship is an opportunity for self-discovery, learning, and growth, and by embracing and adapting to a new culture, you will gain a wealth of invaluable experiences that will shape your future career path.

Gaining Global Perspectives and Building a Global Network

In today's interconnected world, gaining global perspectives and building a global network has become increasingly important for students and interns seeking professional success. Whether you are pursuing an internship, a summer internship, an international internship, or even a remote internship, expanding your horizons and connecting with professionals from around the world can greatly enhance your career prospects.

One of the key benefits of embarking on a global internship is the exposure to different cultures, work environments, and business practices. By immersing yourself in a foreign country or working remotely with an international team, you will develop a broader understanding of how businesses operate on a global scale. This firsthand experience will allow you to adapt more easily to diverse work settings, communicate effectively across cultures, and navigate the complexities of international business.

Additionally, participating in a global internship provides you with the opportunity to build a diverse and expansive network of professionals. Connecting with individuals from different countries and backgrounds can open doors to new career opportunities, collaborations, and mentorship relationships. By actively engaging with your colleagues and supervisors during your internship, you can forge meaningful connections that may prove invaluable throughout your professional journey.

To make the most of your global internship experience, it is crucial to be proactive in seeking out opportunities for cross-cultural learning and networking. Take the initiative to immerse yourself in the local culture, explore the city or region where you are based, and engage in activities that facilitate interaction with locals and fellow interns. Attend professional networking events, join international student organizations, and leverage social media platforms to connect with professionals in your field of interest.

Furthermore, remember that building a global network is a continuous process that extends beyond the duration of your internship. Stay in touch with the connections you make, share updates on your career progress, and offer support whenever possible. By nurturing these relationships, you will create a strong foundation for a global network that can help you throughout your professional journey.

Gaining global perspectives and building a global network through internships, including summer internships, international internships, and remote internships, is an invaluable asset for students and interns. By embracing different cultures, adapting to diverse work settings, and actively networking with professionals from around the world, you will position yourself for long-term professional success in an increasingly globalized job market.

As I also said in the beginning, it's essential to mention that an international internship is no longer just a dream. Even if you have financial constraints and cannot travel, you can still explore the option of remote international internships. With the rise of remote work, many companies are open to offering internships that can be done from the comfort of your home. As long as you can provide value to their organization and align your research or work hours with theirs, they may be more than willing to offer you an international experience. So, don't lose heart if you can't afford to travel abroad for an internship. When applying, inquire about remote internship options, as the international exposure and experience matter more than being physically present in a foreign office.

Nonetheless, specific best practices come into play when pursuing a remote internship, whether it's within your own country or in a foreign land like an international internship. The approach to remote internships differs from traditional methods due to the current dynamics and evolving factors. In the next chapter, we will delve into the realm of remote internships, dissecting the ins and outs. So, let's gear up and prepare ourselves for a more comprehensive understanding.

Chapter 5

Thriving in Remote Internships

Embracing the Remote Work Culture

Nowadays, a new way of talking about things has entered our lives. This new way uses 'pre-COVID' and 'post-COVID' as references. We never thought about this happening before, but now it's real. Perhaps, COVID-19 has become one of the most important events in our lives. People from every generation have seen how it changes our everyday lives, making it a big point to refer to. People now often divide events as either before COVID or after COVID to show the change.

We are now going to use the same for our reference point. Everything has been impacted, including the concept of internships. Before COVID-19, remote internships weren't very popular, and one could even say they barely existed.

However, a lot has changed, and this has greatly influenced the approach to internships.

You all have probably experienced working or studying from home due to the pandemic. This new narrative of "from home" has also entered the realm of internships. Organizations have realized that it's not as detrimental as it may have seemed before. Thanks to the developments in many countries, people have easy access to laptops, desktops, and networks like 4G and 5G, enabling them to work or study from home effectively. This positive shift has encouraged organizations to offer remote internships, allowing interns to contribute from their homes.

Over the past few years, there has been significant learning about the concept of remote internships. Both students and organizations have been evolving their approaches. Institutes and universities have also joined in by encouraging students not only to consider in-person internships but also to explore the potential of remote internships. There are advantages and disadvantages, benefits and limitations, all of which we will delve into, study, analyze, and mitigate in this chapter.

In today's fast-paced and interconnected world, the concept of work has evolved significantly. No longer confined to traditional office settings, remote work has emerged as a popular and viable alternative. Embracing the remote work culture has become more important than ever, particularly for students and internship seekers seeking internships, whether they be summer, international, or remote internships. This subchapter explores the benefits, challenges, and strategies for successfully navigating the remote work landscape.

One of the key advantages of remote work is the flexibility it offers. By embracing this culture, students and interns can break free from the constraints of geographical limitations. Remote internships open up a world of opportunities, allowing them to work with organizations located anywhere across the globe. This enables them to gain valuable cross-cultural experiences, broaden their skillset, and develop a global mindset – all of which are highly sought after in today's competitive job market.

However, embracing the remote work culture also comes with its fair share of challenges. Communication and collaboration can be more complex when working remotely, as face-to-face interactions are limited. Overcoming these challenges requires effective communication skills, adaptability, and the ability to leverage technology tools. It is essential for students and interns to learn how to effectively manage their time, set realistic goals, and maintain a healthy work-life balance in the absence of a physical office environment.

To succeed in remote internships, it is crucial to develop certain strategies. Building strong relationships with supervisors and colleagues through regular communication is essential. Proactive engagement, asking for feedback, and seeking opportunities to contribute beyond assigned tasks can help interns stand out in a remote work setting. Additionally, taking advantage of online resources, virtual networking events, and professional development opportunities can further enhance their skills and expand their professional network.

Embracing the remote work culture offers numerous benefits for students and interns embarking on internship experiences. By adapting to this new way of working, they can gain valuable skills, broaden their horizons, and increase their employability. However, it is important to acknowledge and overcome the unique challenges inherent in remote work, such as effective communication and time management. By implementing the strategies outlined in this subchapter, students and interns can successfully navigate the remote work landscape, making the most of their internship opportunities and positioning themselves for professional success.

Post Covid Era Impact

The rise in popularity of remote internships has been remarkable, primarily attributed to the far-reaching effects of the COVID-19 pandemic. The global outbreak prompted businesses across the world to reconfigure their operations for remote work arrangements, ensuring seamless continuity. Consequently, conventional in-person internships swiftly transformed into remote counterparts, enabling companies to sustain valuable learning avenues for students while also safeguarding their talent pipelines. This shift has not only brought about a paradigm shift in the internship sphere but has also reshaped perspectives concerning remote work and virtual internships.

One of the primary reasons for the growing popularity of remote internships is the accessibility they offer to a diverse pool of candidates. Geographical barriers that previously limited students' opportunities to intern with specific companies are no longer as restrictive in a remote work environment. As internships became virtual, students from different regions and even countries could now participate, enhancing inclusivity and diversity in the workplace.

Moreover, remote internships have proven to be cost-effective for both students and companies. Interns can save on commuting expenses and accommodation costs, while companies can optimize resources and office space. This financial advantage has made remote internships an attractive option for organizations, particularly those that had to adapt to remote work during the pandemic.

In the post-COVID era, the perception of remote internships has significantly evolved. Initially seen as a temporary solution during the pandemic, remote work, including internships, has gained acceptance as a viable and sustainable practice. The successful implementation of remote work models throughout the pandemic demonstrated that productivity and efficiency could be maintained even outside the traditional office setting.

Remote internships have become synonymous with adaptability and resilience, two qualities highly sought after in today's ever-changing job market. Students who have experienced virtual internships have demonstrated their ability to thrive in dynamic and remote environments, making them more attractive to future employers.

Another perception shift is the acknowledgment of remote internships' potential for providing invaluable digital skills. Remote work demands proficiency in virtual collaboration tools, time management, and self-discipline. These skills have become increasingly essential in the modern workplace, making remote internships a prime opportunity for students to develop and showcase these competencies.

Overall, the pandemic accelerated the adoption of remote work and, by extension, remote internships. As the world gradually moves into a post-COVID era, remote internships are likely to remain a prominent and accepted feature of the internship landscape. Their newfound popularity stems from their accessibility, cost-effectiveness, and the recognition of their role in developing critical digital skills. As remote work continues to evolve, remote internships will continue to shape the future of work and learning, opening doors to a more inclusive and diverse workforce.

Researching and Applying for Remote Internships

In today's fast-paced world, the opportunities for internships have expanded beyond the traditional office setting. With advancements in technology and the rise of remote work, students and interns now have the chance to gain valuable experience and develop their skills through remote internships. Whether you are looking for an internship during the summer or seeking an international experience, remote internships offer a flexible and accessible way to kickstart your professional journey.

When it comes to researching remote internships, the internet is your best friend. Start by exploring reputable internship platforms and websites that specialize in remote opportunities. These platforms often curate a wide range of remote internships from various industries and provide detailed descriptions of the positions available. Additionally, consider reaching out to your university's career services office, as they may have connections with companies offering remote internships or can provide guidance on where to search.

It's crucial to thoroughly research the companies or organizations offering remote internships. Take the time to review their websites, social media profiles, and any available reviews or testimonials. This will give you an understanding of their mission, values, and overall reputation. Look for internships that align with your interests, skills, and long-term career goals. Consider the type of work you would like to be involved in and the skills you want to develop during the internship.

The application process for remote internships is often similar to traditional internships. Prepare an updated resume, tailored to highlight relevant skills and experiences. Craft a compelling cover letter that explains why you are interested in the company and how your skills can contribute to their goals. Be sure to emphasize your ability to work independently, manage time effectively, and communicate efficiently in a remote work environment.

When applying for remote internships, it is essential to showcase your adaptability and self-motivation. Highlight any previous remote work experience or examples that demonstrate your ability to work effectively in a virtual setting. Additionally, consider including any relevant technical skills or certifications that may be required for the internship.

Remember to follow up on your applications and be proactive in seeking opportunities. Attend virtual career fairs or networking events specific to remote internships, and connect with professionals in your desired industry on platforms like LinkedIn. Building relationships and making connections can often lead to valuable internship opportunities.

In summary, the world of internships has evolved, and remote internships offer an exciting and flexible way to gain valuable experience. By thoroughly researching and applying for remote internships that align with your goals, you can embark on a professional journey that will set you up for success in the future.

Developing Effective Remote Work Habits

In today's fast-paced and interconnected world, remote work has become increasingly popular, offering students and interns the opportunity to gain valuable experience through internships, summer internships, international internships, and remote internships. However, working remotely requires a different set of skills and habits to ensure productivity and success. This subchapter will guide you in developing effective remote work habits to maximize your potential and achieve professional success.

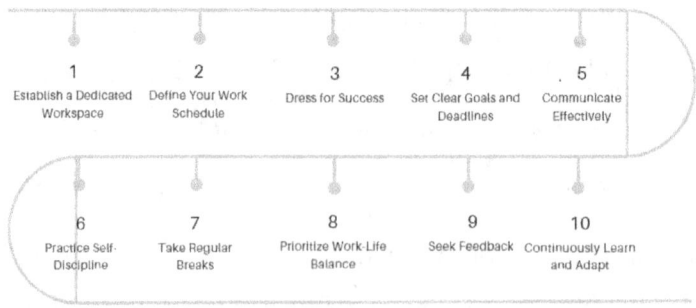

1. **Establish a Dedicated Workspace:** Set up a designated area for work that is free from distractions. This will help you stay focused and create a conducive environment for productivity.

2. **Define Your Work Schedule:** Establish a consistent work schedule that aligns with your internship requirements. This will help you maintain a routine and manage your time effectively.

3. **Dress for Success:** Although working remotely allows for a more relaxed dress code, dressing professionally can help you get into the right mindset and maintain a professional image during virtual meetings.

4. **Set Clear Goals and Deadlines:** Clearly define your goals and break them down into smaller, manageable tasks. Set deadlines for each task to maintain accountability and stay on track.

5. **Communicate Effectively:** Remote work heavily relies on communication, so it is crucial to communicate clearly and efficiently. Utilize digital tools, such as email, video conferencing, and instant messaging, to stay connected with your team and supervisors.

6. **Practice Self-Discipline:** Working remotely requires self-motivation and discipline. Avoid distractions, such as social

media or personal phone calls, during work hours. Stay focused on your tasks and maintain a strong work ethic.

7. **Take Regular Breaks**: It's important to incorporate regular breaks into your workday to recharge and avoid burnout. Get up, stretch, and take short walks to refresh your mind and increase productivity.

8. **Prioritize Work-Life Balance**: Remote work can blur the line between work and personal life. Establish boundaries and set aside time for activities outside of work to maintain a healthy work-life balance and I am saying this from my own experience.

9. **Seek Feedback and Learn from Mistakes:** Actively seek feedback from your supervisors and colleagues to improve your performance. Embrace constructive criticism and use it as an opportunity for growth.

10. **Continuously Learn and Adapt:** Remote work environments are constantly evolving. Stay updated with the latest technology, tools, and best practices to ensure you remain competitive and adaptable in the ever-changing professional landscape.

By implementing these effective remote work habits, you will be able to navigate the challenges and capitalize on the opportunities that arise during your internship, summer internship, international internship, or remote internship. Developing these habits will not only enhance your productivity and professional success but also equip you with valuable skills that can be applied to future remote work opportunities.

Building Strong Communication and Collaboration Skills

Effective communication and collaboration are essential skills that can contribute greatly to your success in any professional setting. Whether you are embarking on an internship, summer internship, international internship, or remote internship, developing these skills will not only enhance your experience but also pave the way for a promising career.

In the modern world where things move quickly and everyone is connected, employers really value the skill of being able to talk and work well with others. This part of the chapter will give you some simple and helpful ideas to make your communication and teamwork skills better. These skills will help you do great during your internship and even in the future.

One of the key aspects of effective communication is active listening. Often overlooked, this skill is crucial for understanding instructions, clarifying expectations, and building strong relationships with colleagues and supervisors. By being fully present in conversations, maintaining eye contact, and asking thoughtful questions, you can demonstrate your engagement and willingness to learn.

Another important element of communication is being able to articulate your thoughts and ideas clearly and concisely. This subchapter will guide you through techniques to improve your verbal and written communication skills, such as organizing your thoughts, using appropriate language, and adapting your communication style to different audiences.

Collaboration skills are equally vital in today's work environment, where teamwork and cooperation are highly valued. You will learn how to effectively contribute to group projects, resolve conflicts, and leverage the strengths of your team members. Additionally, this subchapter will provide guidance on leveraging technology and virtual collaboration tools for successful remote internships, ensuring effective communication despite physical distance.

Remember, strong communication and collaboration skills are not limited to your internship experience; they are transferable skills that will serve you well in any professional setting. By developing these skills early on, you will position yourself as a valuable asset to any team or organization and increase your chances of professional success in the long run.

Chapter 6

Maximizing Your Professional Growth During Internships

Let's approach this chapter from a different perspective to truly grasp its value and significance. Allow me to share a brief anecdote, a story that will shed light on what might be missing or what could be improved upon. Through this story, we will uncover essential insights that can guide us as we delve into this chapter. By learning from this narrative, we can avoid repeating the same mistakes and enhance our understanding. The information within this chapter aims to ensure that we don't find ourselves in the same situation as Alex, enabling us to make more informed choices.

Once upon a time in the bustling city of Metropolis, lived a young and ambitious college graduate named Alex. With dreams as big as the city skyscrapers, Alex had secured an internship at a prestigious tech firm called InnovateTech. It was a golden opportunity for him to kickstart his professional career.

On his first day, Alex was brimming with excitement. He met his fellow interns, attended orientation sessions, and got to know the company's cutting-edge projects. Amidst all the buzz, he was introduced to his mentor, Sarah, a seasoned professional at InnovateTech.

Days turned into weeks, and Alex was enjoying the glamorous life of a tech intern. He attended seminars, workshops, and networking events. He socialized with the company's top executives, and his LinkedIn connections skyrocketed. While his networking game was strong, his actual work seemed to lag behind.

Assigned tasks piled up on Alex's desk, yet he remained preoccupied with building his professional connections. Sarah, his mentor, noticed this and decided to have a candid conversation with him. "Alex, it's great that you're networking, but remember, the real value lies in the work you deliver," she advised him.

Brushing aside her advice, Alex continued to attend conferences and workshops, often missing deadlines for his assignments. The realization that he was falling behind hit him only when he received a less-than-stellar performance review mid-way through the internship.

As the internship neared its end, Alex finally understood the gravity of his situation. He hadn't fully utilized the opportunity to learn, grow, and prove his skills. The very projects he had seen during his orientation could have been his learning ground, but he had underestimated their significance.

With only a few weeks left, Alex was determined to make amends. He approached Sarah, admitted his mistake, and asked for guidance. With Sarah's help, he tackled his projects head-on, staying up late and putting in extra hours. He was determined to showcase his abilities before it was too late.

As the internship concluded, Alex had made significant progress, but it was evident that he had missed out on maximizing his potential. His networking prowess had opened doors, but it was his actual work that would have spoken volumes about his skills. While he did manage to turn the situation around, he knew he could have achieved so much more if he had taken the internship seriously from the start.

The story of Alex serves as a reminder that internships are not just about networking and connections; they are about demonstrating your abilities, contributing to projects, and learning from experienced professionals. Sometimes, underestimating the value of the hands-on experience can lead to missed chances for personal and professional growth.

Setting Clear Objectives for Your Internship

When embarking on an internship, it is crucial to establish clear objectives to make the most out of this valuable opportunity. By setting specific goals, you can maximize your learning experience, gain practical skills, and pave the way for future success. This subchapter will guide you through the process of setting clear objectives for your internship, regardless of whether it is a summer internship, international internship, or remote internship.

First and foremost, take the time to reflect on your personal and professional aspirations. What are your areas of interest? What skills do you want to develop? By understanding your own goals, you can align them with the objectives of your internship. For instance, if you are interested in marketing, you may set an objective to improve your social media management skills or learn about market research techniques.

Next, consider the expectations of your internship program or supervisor. Meet with your supervisor to discuss their expectations and clarify what they hope you will achieve during your time with them. This will help you align your objectives with their goals, ensuring that you are working towards a common purpose.

Once you have a clear understanding of your own goals and the expectations of your internship, it is time to set specific objectives. Make sure your objectives are measurable and realistic. For example, instead of setting a vague objective like "improve communication skills," you might set a more specific objective such as "deliver a presentation to a team of colleagues by the end of the internship.

It is essential to break down your objectives into smaller, manageable tasks. This will help you stay focused and track your progress throughout the internship. Consider creating a timeline or action plan to ensure that you are working towards your objectives effectively.

Lastly, regularly evaluate your progress and make adjustments as needed. Check in with your supervisor or mentor to receive feedback and guidance. This will help you stay on track and make any necessary improvements to achieve your objectives.

By setting clear objectives for your internship, you will transform this experience into a stepping stone towards your professional success. Whether you are pursuing a summer internship, international internship, or remote internship, the process of setting objectives remains the same. Take the time to define your goals, align them with the expectations of your internship, and break them down into actionable tasks. With a clear roadmap in place, you will make the most of your internship and gain valuable skills for your future career.

Cultivating a Positive and Professional Attitude

In today's competitive job market, having technical skills and knowledge is important, but it's equally crucial to develop a positive and professional attitude. This subchapter will explore the significance of cultivating this mindset during your internship journey, regardless of whether it is a summer internship, international internship, or remote internship.

A positive attitude is the foundation of success. It not only affects your own experience but also influences how others perceive you. When you approach your internship with enthusiasm and optimism, you create a welcoming and productive environment for yourself and your colleagues. A positive attitude allows you to adapt to new challenges, learn from feedback, and showcase your potential as a valuable team member.

Maintaining professionalism throughout your internship is equally essential. This means conducting yourself with integrity, respect, and accountability. Remember, you are building your professional reputation, and every interaction and task contributes to that. Demonstrating professionalism includes dressing appropriately, arriving on time, meeting deadlines, and communicating effectively. These behaviours showcase your commitment and reliability, setting you apart from other interns.

Being professional also means taking initiative and going the extra mile. Seek opportunities to contribute beyond your assigned tasks, offer assistance to colleagues, and show a willingness to learn. By demonstrating initiative, you display your dedication to personal and professional growth. This mindset not only benefits your internship experience but also lays the foundation for future career success.

Additionally, cultivating a positive and professional attitude can enhance your networking opportunities. Building relationships with professionals in your field is crucial for future job prospects. A positive attitude attracts others and makes you more approachable. People are more likely to remember and recommend someone who has a positive impact on their work environment.

To foster a positive and professional attitude, it is essential to take care of yourself. Prioritize self-care, manage stress effectively, and seek opportunities for personal growth. This will help you maintain a positive mindset and handle the challenges that may arise during your internship.

In conclusion, cultivating a positive and professional attitude is a fundamental aspect of your internship journey. It not only enhances your own experience but also impacts your professional growth and networking opportunities. By approaching your internship with enthusiasm, professionalism, and a commitment to personal development, you are setting yourself up for long-term success in your chosen career path.

Building Strong Relationships with Colleagues and Mentors

In today's competitive job market, internships have become a crucial stepping stone for students and interns to gain practical experience and develop professional skills. However, internships are not just about completing tasks and adding a line to your resume. They also offer a unique opportunity to build strong relationships with colleagues and mentors, which can significantly impact your career trajectory. (However, I want to make a point clear. When I mention networking and building relationships with colleagues and executives, I don't mean just adding more connections on LinkedIn. The goal is to establish genuine, meaningful connections that provide support and mentorship, rather than using them for mere show-off on social media platforms.)

One of the most valuable aspects of an internship is the chance to work alongside experienced professionals who can provide guidance and mentorship. Mentors can offer invaluable insights into the industry, share their experiences, and provide advice on navigating the professional world. Establishing a strong rapport with your mentor can open doors to new opportunities, such as recommendations for future job prospects or even potential collaborations on projects.

To build a solid relationship with your mentor, it is essential to demonstrate enthusiasm, curiosity, and a willingness to learn. Actively seek feedback and guidance, showing that you value their expertise. Engage in conversations about industry trends, seek their opinion on your work, and ask for constructive criticism to improve your skills.

In addition to mentors, cultivating relationships with colleagues is equally important during an internship. Colleagues can offer a support network, provide insights into the company culture, and help you navigate through any challenges that may arise during your internship.

To foster strong relationships with colleagues, it is crucial to be a team player and contribute to the overall success of the organization. Offer assistance to your colleagues when they need it, be proactive in taking on additional responsibilities, and show a willingness to collaborate. Participating in team-building activities or social events can also help strengthen bonds with your colleagues outside of the office environment.

In the case of remote internships or international internships, building relationships may present unique challenges. However, technology has made it easier than ever to connect with colleagues and mentors from a distance. Take advantage of video conferencing tools, instant messaging platforms, and social media to stay connected and engage in meaningful conversations.

Remember, internships are not just about the tasks you complete or the projects you work on. They are also an opportunity to build a network of professionals who can support and guide you throughout your career. By investing time and effort in building strong relationships with colleagues and mentors, you can maximize the benefits of your internship and set yourself up for professional success.

Developing Essential Skills and Acquiring New Knowledge

In today's competitive job market, internships have become a crucial stepping stone towards professional success. Whether you are a student, trainee, or recent graduate, internships provide an invaluable opportunity to gain hands-on experience, develop essential skills, and acquire new knowledge in your desired field. This subchapter aims to guide you through the process of maximizing your internship experience and transforming it into a launching pad for your future career.

Internships offer a unique learning environment that goes beyond theoretical knowledge gained in the classroom. They provide practical exposure to real-world challenges, allowing you to apply your academic learning to practical scenarios. This hands-on experience enables you to develop essential skills that are highly sought after by employers. Skills such as communication, teamwork, problem-solving, and adaptability are all honed during an internship, setting you apart from your peers in the job market.

Additionally, internships offer the opportunity to acquire new knowledge and expand your understanding of the industry you are interested in. By immersing yourself in the day-to-day operations of a company, you gain insights into various aspects of the industry, such as trends, challenges, and best practices. This knowledge not only enhances your employability but also allows you to make informed decisions about your future career path.

This subchapter addresses the different types of internships available, catering to students' diverse needs and interests. Whether you are looking for a summer internship, an international experience, or a remote opportunity, it provides guidance on finding and securing the right internship for you. It highlights the benefits and challenges associated with each type of internship, equipping you with the necessary information to make an informed decision.

Moreover, this subchapter delves into practical strategies to make the most of your internship experience. It provides advice on setting goals and expectations, seeking feedback, networking, and leveraging your internship to build a strong professional network. It emphasizes the importance of taking initiative, being proactive, and continuously learning during your internship journey.

Internships are an invaluable opportunity for students to develop essential skills and acquire new knowledge. This subchapter aims to guide you through the process of maximizing your internship experience, whether it be a summer internship, an international experience, or a remote opportunity. By following the strategies outlined in this subchapter, you can transform your internship into a stepping stone towards professional success.

Leveraging Internship Success for Future Career Opportunities

Internships have become an essential stepping stone towards a successful career. They offer students and interns the opportunity to gain practical experience, develop valuable skills, and build a professional network. However, the benefits of internships extend far beyond the immediate job placement. By leveraging your internship success, you can open doors to future career opportunities that may have seemed out of reach.

One of the key ways to leverage your internship success is by actively seeking feedback and using it to improve your skills. During your internship, take the initiative to ask for feedback from your supervisors and colleagues. Use this feedback to identify areas of improvement and work on them. By demonstrating a willingness to learn and grow, you will position yourself as a valuable asset to future employers.

Another way to leverage your internship success is by building and nurturing your professional network. Networking is a powerful tool that can open doors to hidden job opportunities. Connect with professionals in your field, attend industry events, and utilize online platforms like LinkedIn to expand your network. Maintain relationships with your internship mentors and colleagues, as they can serve as valuable references and provide recommendations for future positions.

Additionally, showcasing your internship experience on your resume and during job interviews is crucial. Tailor your resume to highlight the skills and experiences gained during your internship. Quantify your achievements and provide specific examples of how you contributed to the success of the organization. During interviews, articulate how your internship experience has prepared you for the role and demonstrate your ability to apply your skills in a professional setting.

For students interested in internships leveraging your internship success becomes even more important. Summer internships provide a condensed work experience and can be a gateway to full-time positions. International internships offer the opportunity to gain a global perspective and develop cross-cultural skills. Remote internships allow you to demonstrate your ability to work independently and remotely, which is becoming increasingly important in today's digital age.

In summary, Internships are not just temporary work experiences but valuable stepping stones towards future career opportunities. By actively seeking feedback, building your professional network, showcasing your internship experience, and targeting specific internship niches, you can leverage your internship success to open doors and propel your professional journey forward. Remember, it's not just about the internship itself, but how you use it to shape your future.

Chapter 7

Overcoming Challenges and Obstacles in Internships

Dealing with Work Pressure and Deadlines

This is where theory meets reality. The entire purpose of doing an internship is to experience a real work culture. Depending on the situation and company dynamics, your experience could be unique compared to others. However, it is essential to embrace this uniqueness. For freshers, it includes everything from understanding outcome expectations to immersing themselves in the work environment.

Don't take it lightly; instead, try to enjoy every aspect of it. The more you enjoy, the better you adapt to the work culture, and the more prepared you become for your future job. This experience holds significant importance for your career growth.

Each of us possesses a distinct and individual personality. What may be a weakness for me could be a strength for you, and vice versa. This diversity leads to unique challenges and problems during your internship program. Every student is bound to encounter certain challenges during their internship journey. The significance of these challenges hinges entirely on your personality and your approach to handling them. These challenges could span various areas, such as communication issues, navigating organizational dynamics, team politics, clashes of ego, seeking attention, or even working comfortably across genders. As I mentioned, these challenges can be quite personal, but it's crucial to find solutions. In this chapter, I'll discuss some of the commonly known problems that arise during internships, how to approach them, and how to seek support. This knowledge will hopefully boost your confidence when facing such situations during your internship.

Managing Work Pressure

Let's now deal with one of the most challenging aspects of any internship is the ability to handle work pressure and meet strict deadlines. As a student or trainee, it is important to develop effective strategies to cope with these demands in order to succeed in your internship and pave your path to professional success. This subchapter will guide you through essential tips and techniques to thrive under work pressure and meet deadlines, regardless of whether you are engaged in an internship, summer internship, international internship, or remote internship.

Firstly, it is crucial to manage your time effectively. Create a schedule or to-do list that outlines your tasks and priorities for each day. Break down larger projects into smaller, manageable tasks, and allocate specific time slots for each task. This will help you stay organized and ensure that you are making progress towards your goals. Additionally, be sure to set realistic deadlines for yourself, allowing ample time for unexpected delays or revisions.

Another key strategy is to maintain open communication with your supervisor or mentor. If you are feeling overwhelmed with the workload or struggling to meet a deadline, don't hesitate to reach out for guidance or assistance. Your superiors are there to support you and are often willing to provide additional resources or adjust timelines if necessary.

Furthermore, it is important to take care of yourself both mentally and physically. Engage in stress-relieving activities such as exercise, meditation, or hobbies that help you relax and recharge. Ensure that you are getting enough sleep and eating well-balanced meals to sustain your energy levels. Remember, taking care of yourself is essential for maintaining focus and productivity.

Lastly, embrace the power of prioritization. Evaluate the urgency and importance of each task and focus on high-priority items first. By tackling the most critical tasks early on, you will alleviate stress and create a sense of accomplishment, motivating you to continue with other assignments.

Managing work pressure and meeting deadlines are essential skills for success in any internship or professional setting. By implementing effective time management techniques, maintaining open communication, prioritizing tasks, and taking care of your well-being, you will be better equipped to handle the demands of your internship. Remember, it is through overcoming challenges that you grow both personally and professionally, and your ability to excel under pressure will significantly contribute to your future success.

Managing Conflicts and Resolving Issues

In the fast-paced and dynamic world of internships, conflicts and issues are bound to arise. Whether you are participating in a summer internship, international internship, or even a remote internship, it is essential to develop the skills to effectively manage conflicts and resolve issues that may arise during your professional journey. This subchapter aims to

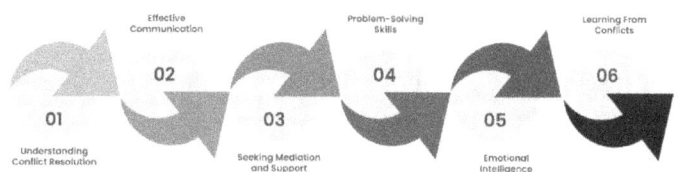

provide you with valuable insights and strategies to navigate these challenges successfully.

1. **Understanding Conflict Resolution**: Conflict is a natural part of any workplace environment. It is crucial to understand the various styles of conflict resolution, such as compromising, collaborating, or accommodating. By recognizing your own conflict resolution style and adapting it to different situations, you can better address conflicts and reach mutually beneficial outcomes.

2. **Effective Communication**: Communication is key to resolving conflicts. As an intern, it is vital to express your thoughts and concerns in a clear and respectful manner. Active listening is equally important, allowing you to understand different perspectives and find common ground. Miscommunication can often escalate conflicts, so always strive to maintain open and honest lines of communication.

3. **Seeking Mediation and Support:** If a conflict becomes too challenging to handle on your own, do not hesitate to seek mediation or support from your supervisor, mentor, or human resources department. They can provide guidance, facilitate discussions, and help find a resolution that satisfies all parties involved.

4. **Problem-Solving Skills:** Developing strong problem-solving skills is essential for resolving issues. By breaking down the problem into manageable parts, brainstorming possible solutions, and evaluating the pros and cons of each option, you can come up with effective strategies to overcome challenges.

5. **Emotional Intelligence:** Emotions can often run high during conflicts, making it crucial to develop emotional intelligence. This includes recognizing and managing your own emotions, as well as empathizing with others. By staying calm, composed, and respectful, you can foster a positive environment that encourages constructive conflict resolution.

6. **Learning From Conflicts:** Conflicts and issues can provide valuable learning opportunities. Take the time to reflect on each conflict and identify areas for personal growth and improvement. By learning from these experiences, you can

enhance your professional skills and become better equipped to handle future challenges.

In short, managing conflicts and resolving issues is an essential skill set for any intern, regardless of the type of internship. By understanding conflict resolution styles, practicing effective communication, seeking support when needed, honing problem-solving skills, and developing emotional intelligence, you can navigate conflicts successfully and pave the way for professional success. Remember, conflicts are not obstacles but opportunities for growth and improvement.

Handling Feedback and Criticism

Receiving feedback and criticism is an integral part of personal and professional growth. As an intern, you will encounter various situations where feedback and criticism will play a crucial role in shaping your skills and performance. This subchapter will guide you on how to effectively handle feedback and criticism, allowing you to leverage these experiences for your professional success.

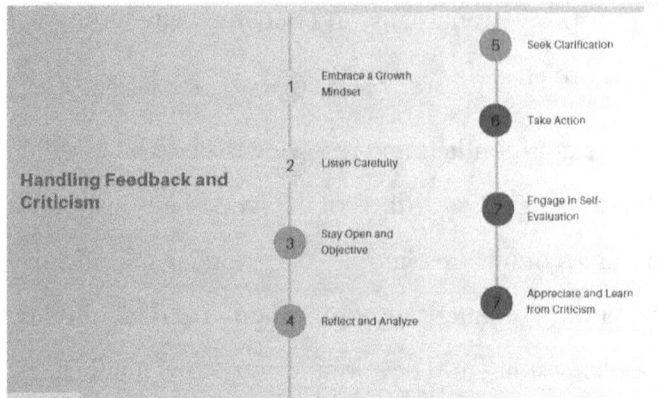

1. **Embrace a Growth Mindset:** Understand that feedback and criticism are opportunities for improvement, not personal attacks. Adopting a growth mindset will help you approach feedback with an open mind and a willingness to learn.

2. **Listen Carefully:** When receiving feedback, actively listen to the person providing it. Pay attention to their words, tone, and non-verbal cues. Demonstrate your commitment to understanding their perspective by asking clarifying questions.

3. **Stay Open and Objective:** Avoid becoming defensive or taking feedback personally. Instead, view it as an opportunity to gain valuable insights into your strengths and areas for improvement. Maintain objectivity and consider the feedback from a professional standpoint.

4. **Reflect and Analyze:** Take time to reflect on the feedback you receive. Consider the validity of the comments and identify areas where you can make changes or improvements. Self-reflection is essential for growth and development.

5. **Seek Clarification:** If you are unsure about certain aspects of the feedback or would like more information, don't hesitate to ask for clarification. Engage in a constructive dialogue with the person providing feedback and gain a deeper understanding of their perspective.

6. **Take Action:** Use the feedback as a catalyst for improvement. Develop an action plan to address the identified areas for growth. Proactively seek opportunities to implement the feedback and demonstrate your commitment to growth.

7. **Engage in Self-Evaluation:** Regularly assess your own performance and seek feedback from mentors and supervisors. This self-evaluation will help you identify areas for improvement and demonstrate your dedication to personal and professional growth.

8. **Appreciate and Learn from Criticism:** Understand that criticism can be a valuable tool for learning and development. Embrace it as an opportunity to enhance your skills and

become a better professional. Appreciate those who provide constructive criticism, as they are invested in your success.

Handling feedback and criticism is an essential skill for any intern. By adopting a growth mindset, actively listening, reflecting, and taking action, you can transform feedback into a powerful tool for personal and professional growth. Embrace these opportunities, and they will pave the way for your success in internships, whether they are summer internships, international internships, or remote internships.

Balancing Work and Personal Life

We discussed this aspect during remote internships, but failing to balance work and personal life can lead to negative outcomes, regardless of the type of internship. I have my own experience in this regard. It wasn't great initially, but later on, I managed it better. Everyone has their own learning curve, and you grasp things through your own experiences, no matter how much advice or guidance you receive.

The significance of maintaining a work-life balance changes and evolves as you grow older – and I'm not joking, this is truly how it happens. When you're young, full of energy, and have ample time, you're enthusiastic about working hard and putting in long hours to achieve your goals. However, as life introduces new elements like relationships, friends, or family, your priorities tend to shift.

You make efforts to adjust and find a balance between your personal life and work commitments. Often, personal life takes precedence over work during these times. This pattern may continue for a while. However, as time passes, especially when you have a family with a spouse and children, you come to realize the true importance of work-life balance.

As you age, your health and energy levels may not be the same as they used to be. This is a natural progression. This realization often leads to valuing work-life balance more prominently. Sometimes, this realization comes later than expected, and that's why it's crucial to prioritize "work-life balance" right from the start.

So, my dear friends, why delay? Let's adopt healthy practices right from the beginning.

But finding a healthy balance between work and personal life can be a challenge as a student. As students and interns, navigating the demands of internships, whether they are summer, international, or remote, can make achieving this balance seem even more daunting. However, with the right mindset and strategies, it is possible to successfully manage both aspects of your life and thrive in your internship experience.

The first step towards achieving a work-life balance is understanding your priorities. It is crucial to identify what matters most to you in both your professional and personal life. Are you looking to gain valuable skills and experience during your internship? Or maybe you want to maintain strong relationships with family and friends? Once you have a clear understanding of your priorities, you can allocate your time and energy accordingly.

Setting boundaries is another essential aspect of maintaining a healthy work-life balance. As an intern, it is easy to get caught up in the excitement of your new role and feel obligated to work longer hours or take on additional tasks. While dedication is commendable, it is important to recognize that burning out will ultimately hinder your progress. Set realistic expectations with your supervisors and colleagues about your availability and workload, and communicate openly if you feel overwhelmed. This will not only protect your personal life but also ensure that you can perform at your best in your internship.

Additionally, incorporating self-care practices into your daily routine is crucial. Take time to engage in activities that rejuvenate you, whether it's exercising, reading, or spending quality time with loved ones. Remember that self-care is not a luxury but a necessity for your mental, emotional, and physical well-being. By prioritizing self-care, you will be better equipped to handle the demands of your internship while maintaining a sense of balance.

Lastly, don't be afraid to ask for support when needed. Reach out to mentors, fellow interns, or your support network to share your experiences, seek advice, and gain perspective. Their guidance can offer valuable insights and help you navigate any challenges that arise. Remember that you are not alone on this journey, and seeking support is a sign of strength, not weakness.

Finding a balance between work and personal life is an ongoing process that requires continuous evaluation and adjustment. By understanding your priorities, setting boundaries, practicing self-care, and seeking support, you can successfully navigate your internship experience while maintaining a healthy and fulfilling personal life. Remember, achieving a work-life balance is not only beneficial for your internship but also essential for your long-term personal and professional success.

Maintaining Motivation and Resilience

Maintaining motivation and resilience is essential for students and interns seeking professional success. Whether you are embarking on a summer internship, international internship, or remote internship, this subchapter will provide valuable guidance on how to stay motivated and resilient throughout your journey.

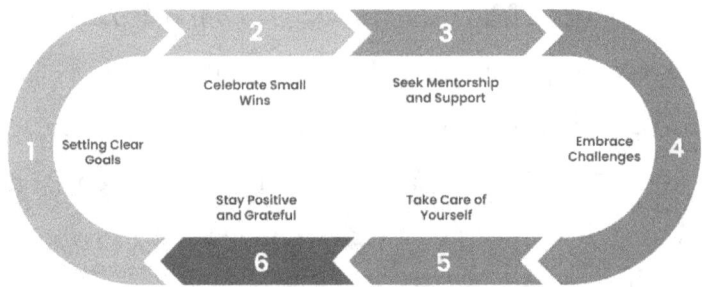

1. Setting Clear Goals: One of the key factors in maintaining motivation is setting clear and achievable goals. Start by identifying what you hope to achieve during your internship, whether it's gaining specific skills, networking with professionals in your field, or completing a project. By having a roadmap of your objectives, you will be more motivated to work towards them.

2. **Celebrate Small Wins**: Acknowledging and celebrating your accomplishments along the way is crucial for staying motivated. Remember to reward yourself for completing tasks or achieving milestones during your internship. This positive reinforcement will keep you motivated and eager to take on new challenges.

3. **Seek Mentorship and Support**: Building a network of mentors and colleagues who can provide guidance and support is essential for resilience. Reach out to professionals in your field of interest and ask for their advice or mentorship. Having someone to turn to during challenging times will help you stay motivated and bounce back from setbacks.

4. **Embrace Challenges**: Internships can be demanding and may present unexpected challenges. Instead of viewing these challenges as obstacles, embrace them as opportunities for growth. Adopting a growth mindset will help you stay motivated and resilient, enabling you to overcome obstacles and learn from your experiences.

5. **Take Care of Yourself**: Self-care is crucial for maintaining motivation and resilience. Make sure to prioritize your physical and mental well-being during your internship journey. Get enough sleep, eat a balanced diet, exercise regularly, and engage in activities that bring you joy and

relaxation. By taking care of yourself, you will have the energy and resilience to tackle any challenges that come your way.

6. **Stay Positive and Grateful:** Lastly, maintaining a positive mindset and gratitude for the opportunities you have can greatly impact your motivation and resilience. Focus on the positive aspects of your internship experience, and remind yourself of the valuable skills and experiences you are gaining. By cultivating gratitude, you will be motivated to make the most of your internship and remain resilient in the face of adversity.

Remember, maintaining motivation and resilience is a journey. By following these tips, you will be well-equipped to navigate the ups and downs of your internship, regardless of whether it's a summer internship, international internship, or remote internship. Stay focused, stay positive, and stay determined – your path to professional success starts with maintaining motivation and resilience.

Chapter 8

Transitioning from Internship to Full-Time Employment

The phase of transitioning from an internship to a more permanent role is a crucial juncture that demands a well-defined approach for everyone. This is where some individuals might miss out on valuable opportunities due to the critical nature of the transition. The experience of transitioning can vary depending on the type of internship you are engaged in. If your internship inherently leads to a permanent job, the level of preparedness required is different. On the other hand, if your internship is of a shorter duration and you must move on to a different job or role in another organization, this kind of transition brings its own set of experiences and challenges.

The latter type of transition, where you must depart from the organization after your internship and then search for a job role, is not without its difficulties. I have personally observed that many students face challenges and sometimes give up during this phase of their journey. I will discuss the significance of this transition, highlight why it is crucial, and stress the importance of being well-prepared. By putting in a little extra effort, you can position yourself to secure your dream job. This is my aim: to help every individual who aspires to land their dream job through an internship achieve exactly that.

Evaluating Potential Job Offers

Now you are very close to the corporate reality. When you apply for internships, there are two types: the first one is short-term, where the purpose is to leave the organization after the internship is over. You receive a token of appreciation, a certificate, and your training ends. You are then on your own in the corporate market, and you have to find a job based on what you have learned during your internship.

The second type of internship is offered by the organization to train you in specific aspects. After the successful completion of the internship, you may receive an offer to be absorbed as a permanent employee within the same company.

Right from the beginning, when you apply for an internship, you must figure out whether it is a short-term internship with an exit after completion, or if there's a chance of being absorbed into a full-time job, like many other students hope for. Your priority should be to find an internship that can lead to a seamless transition into a full-time position after completion.

I am confident that when you search for such internships, you will be clear about your goals, the type of company you want to work for, and the organizational culture you wish to adopt. This way, there will be no surprises for you, and your internship experience can potentially turn into a promising job offer.

When it comes to internships, evaluating potential job offers is a crucial step in securing your path to professional success. As students and intern, the decision to accept or decline an offer can have a lasting impact on your career trajectory. In this subchapter, we will explore key factors that should be considered when evaluating internship offers.

Now, let's talk about job offers. There are two kinds of job offers: one is offered to you right after the completion of your internship within the same organization, and the other type is when you are in the open market, apply to different organizations, go through the entire interview and selection process, and then receive a job offer.

In this part of the chapter, we will learn how to evaluate a job offer. After you have completed your internship, gained valuable experience, and now received a job offer, it's essential to assess the offer before making a decision. Take the time to evaluate the job offer and value yourself before accepting it.

Some of you might be thinking that in today's economic situation and such a competitive environment, getting a job itself is a significant achievement. In such a scenario, evaluating and deciding whether the job in hand is suitable for you or not might seem like a big task. Well, it's entirely your choice. If you feel that the first job offer is your dream job, go ahead and grab it. But remember, sometimes the job that was meant for you might be waiting for you, and you might miss out on that opportunity if you don't evaluate other options.

If you want to explore and make an informed decision, I highly recommend evaluating your first job offer thoroughly. Check if it aligns with your expectations, goals, and objectives. Ensure that it sets you on a path for the next 3 to 5 years, leading towards your desired career journey. Evaluating becomes even more crucial because some companies offer you a job right after your internship and may ask you to sign a bond for 1 or 2 years. You certainly don't want to be stuck in a situation where you don't enjoy the job but are bound by the contract. So, take the time to evaluate the job offer carefully.

For those who does not know about signing a bond in the job contract.

In the context of signing an offer letter for a job, a "bond" refers to a contractual agreement between the employer and the employee. This bond typically includes certain terms and conditions that the employee agrees to abide by during their employment with the company. It may require the employee to stay with the company for a specified period, often known as the bond period.

During the bond period, the employee is legally bound to fulfil the terms of the agreement, which may include staying with the company for a minimum duration, undertaking specific projects, or adhering to certain performance expectations. If the employee wishes to leave the company before the bond period expires, they may be required to pay a penalty or compensate the employer as specified in the bond agreement.

Companies may use bonds as a way to retain valuable employees, especially in industries where training and development of employees are significant investments. On the other hand, employees need to carefully consider the terms and implications of the bond before signing the offer letter, as it may impact their future career choices and opportunities.

.When we evaluate a job offer, there are various parameters to consider. One parameter is whether the offered role aligns with your level and if the assigned responsibilities are in line with your goals. Another aspect to assess is whether the job location matches your preferences. Additionally, you need to analyze if the salary or compensation package meet your expectations as stated in the job offer.

I believe all these parameters are crucial, but their importance may vary based on individual preferences. Among them, the compensation part holds significant weight and deserves thorough discussion and analysis.

Now we know that important aspect to consider is the compensation package. While internships may not always come with a high salary, it is crucial to assess the overall benefits and opportunities provided. Look beyond the monetary aspect and consider other perks such as mentorship programs, training initiatives, or the potential for full-time employment after the internship. These additional benefits can greatly impact your overall experience and future job prospects.

In Addition, evaluate the location and work environment of the internship. For international internships, consider the cultural differences, language barriers, and potential for personal growth. Remote internships may offer flexibility and convenience, allowing you to work from the comfort of your home or any location of your choice. These considerations can greatly impact your work-life balance and overall satisfaction during your internship.

Evaluating potential job offers is a critical process in securing a successful internship experience. By assessing factors such as relevance, reputation, compensation, location, and work environment, you can make an informed decision that aligns with your career goals. Remember, internships are not just about gaining experience; they are stepping stones towards professional success.

Navigating the Job Application Process

As we discussed earlier, after completing an internship, you may receive a job offer, either from the same organization where you interned or from the open job market when you actively search for opportunities. Understanding the job application process is crucial, from finding the right job to securing it successfully. Now, let's dive deeper into the details of this job application process for those who couldn't transition their internship into a job. Don't worry, there are still plenty of opportunities awaiting you.

The job application process can be quite overwhelming, especially for students and individuals completed the internships. But fear not, with the right strategies and proper guidance, you can confidently tackle this challenge and secure the job you've always dreamed of. In this section, we will delve into the crucial steps and valuable tips to ensure that your job application shines brightly amidst the competition.

There's another situation that I want to clarify so that there's no confusion. When we talk about job applications, it can happen right after completing your internship or even before applying for an internship. Sometimes, companies advertise a job offer that includes an initial two-month internship component before transitioning into a permanent role. It's essential to understand the difference between the two scenarios, and although the preparation remains similar, you might need to put in some extra effort when applying for a job offer that also includes an internship component.

Firstly, it is crucial to understand the specific requirements and qualifications for the internship you are applying for, as it may also lead to a job offer later. Take the time to carefully read the job description and thoroughly research the organization to gain a comprehensive understanding of their values and goals. Tailor your application to highlight how your skills and experiences align with what the company is seeking. This personalized approach will significantly enhance your chances of landing the internship and potentially securing a job offer in the future.

Crafting a compelling resume and cover letter is equally important. Your resume should be concise, yet informative, highlighting your relevant education, experiences, and accomplishments. Use action verbs and quantify your achievements whenever possible. Your cover letter should be personalized and demonstrate your enthusiasm for the role. Mention specific projects, initiatives, or aspects of the company that resonate with you.

Networking can significantly enhance your job application process. Reach out to professionals in your field of interest, attend career fairs, and engage with alumni from your school. Building connections can lead to valuable insights and potential referrals, increasing your chances of securing an internship.

Another crucial aspect is preparing for interviews. Research commonly asked interview questions and practice your responses. Reflect on your experiences and articulate how they have shaped your skills and abilities. Additionally, be prepared to ask thoughtful questions about the company and the role you are applying for. This shows your genuine interest and eagerness to learn.

For students interested in international or remote internships, additional considerations come into play. Research the cultural norms and expectations of the country you are applying to, as well as any potential visa requirements. For remote internships, focus on highlighting your ability to work independently and communicate effectively through virtual platforms.

Remember, the job application process is a learning experience. Don't be discouraged by rejection; instead, use it as an opportunity to refine your application materials and interview skills. Stay proactive, seek feedback, and continuously improve your approach.

By following these steps, you can successfully navigate the job application process and increase your chances of securing an internship that aligns with your goals and aspirations. Good luck on your journey towards professional success!

Preparing for Job Interviews

Job interviews can be nerve-wracking, especially if it's your first time. However, with the right preparation and mindset, you can turn this intimidating experience into an opportunity to shine. This subchapter will guide you through the essential steps to prepare for job interviews, ensuring that you leave a lasting impression on potential employers.

Research the Company: Before heading into an interview, it is crucial to thoroughly research the company. Familiarize yourself with their mission, values, products, services, and recent news. This knowledge will not only demonstrate your genuine interest but also help you tailor your answers to align with the company's goals and culture.

Review Your Resume: Ensure that you have a clear understanding of the content on your resume. Be ready to elaborate on your experiences, skills, and achievements mentioned in your CV. Prepare specific examples of how you have demonstrated these skills in previous internships, summer internships, or remote internships. This will help you illustrate your qualifications effectively during the interview.

Practice Common Interview Questions: Anticipate and practice responses to commonly asked interview questions. This includes questions about your strengths, weaknesses, previous experiences, and your ability to work in a team. Practice your answers out loud or with a friend to build confidence and ensure that your responses are concise, yet informative. Here is list of some common questions. I encourage you not to resort to memorizing standard responses for interview questions. Each internship experience is distinctive, offering unique insights and learning opportunities. Your responses should reflect this individuality and highlight the aspects specific to your internship.

Consider this task as an assignment stemming from the guidance in this book. Take your time to reflect on your experience and craft your responses accordingly. It's normal to iterate a few times and refine your answers. Seek guidance from others, practice multiple times, and you'll eventually arrive at a well-prepared response.

This practice is important because it helps you prepare for typical questions that companies commonly ask during interviews. Being able to give honest and personalized responses will make you stand out. So, I talked to my friends and colleagues to find out what questions are frequently asked and what are some of the most popular questions interns should be ready for in an interview. Here are a few examples to give you an idea.

- *Question: Can you tell us about your internship experience and the projects you worked on?*
- *Question: What challenges did you encounter during your internship, and how did you handle them?*
- *Question: How did your internship contribute to your professional development and career aspirations?*
- *Question: Can you describe a specific project or task you worked on during your internship that you are particularly proud of?*
- *Question: How do you handle constructive criticism and feedback from your superiors?*
- *Question: What motivates you to excel in your work, and how do you stay motivated during challenging times?*

- *Question: How do you prioritize tasks and manage your time effectively?*

Remember, the key to a successful interview is to be authentic, confident, and showcase your enthusiasm for the role and the company. By preparing thoughtful responses to these commonly asked questions, you can make a strong impression and increase your chances of securing a job offer after completing your internship. Now, let's delve into some of the essential steps that are involved or necessary when preparing for a job interview.

Dress Professionally: Dressing appropriately for an interview is essential even it is remotely done. Research the company's dress code and make sure to present yourself in a manner that reflects their standards. Even if the company has a casual work environment, it is always better to be slightly overdressed than underdressed.

Prepare Questions to Ask: Prepare a list of thoughtful questions to ask the interviewer. This will not only show your genuine interest but also help you assess if the company is the right fit for you. Ask about the company culture, growth opportunities, and the expectations for the position you are applying for.

Mock Interviews: Organize mock interviews with a friend or mentor who can provide constructive feedback. Practice answering questions, maintaining eye contact, and controlling your body language. Mock interviews help you identify and improve upon any weaknesses, ensuring that you are well-prepared for the real interview.

Follow-Up: After the interview, send a personalized thank-you email or note to express your gratitude for the opportunity. Use this opportunity to reiterate your interest in the position and briefly summarize why you would be a valuable addition to their team.

By following these steps, you will be well-prepared and confident for any job interview. Remember, the key is to showcase your skills, experiences, and enthusiasm, while also demonstrating your fit within the company culture. Good luck with your future interviews and your journey towards professional success!

Although I suggested follow-up as one of the last steps in preparing for the interview, based on my experience, and I am sure many others would echo the same sentiment, only a few organizations are so professional that they respond promptly to your emails/calls. The majority of companies and organizations do not bother to provide feedback or respond for the next steps. However, don't be disheartened by this. Some organizations follow poor practices in their hiring process, and it is challenging to pinpoint a specific manager or HR person responsible for these practices.

I can understand that in a high-volume hiring process, it may be challenging for organizations to respond to every single candidate after their interview is completed. However, when the volume is manageable, providing a proper closure to the interview process is crucial to demonstrate great professional behaviour. From the candidate's perspective, imagine applying for a job for the first time, going through the application and interview process, and then not receiving any response about the status. This could create a negative impression, which we want to avoid.

It is essential for us to support each other in this sensitive matter. Personally, I strongly dislike seeing candidates undergo unnecessary stress and uncertainty when awaiting the outcome of their applications. I won't delve into market practices, but I believe we should show care and empathy towards students and the wider community.

Showcasing Internship Experience on Your Resume

In the previous chapters while applying for an internship, we briefly discussed the importance of creating a good resume.

Now, we will delve deeper into this specific subject of creating a resume post internship. Let's quickly recap - when we were applying for the internship, we didn't have any experience, but we had some best practices that we followed to craft our resume.

Now, we have taken a step ahead. We have completed our internship, and we want to apply for job opportunities in the market and approach organizations. But for this, we need to revisit our resume, and this is crucial. We need to present ourselves with a fresh identity because post-internship, many things have changed in our lives. We have learned a lot personally and professionally from our superiors and colleagues, and that is our treasure. It will help us in seeking and securing our desired job. So, it becomes essential to eloquently express our internship experiences using impactful words that will impress the interviewer. Alright, let's dive into more details.

Firstly, rebuilding the resume allows students to emphasize the specific projects, responsibilities, and accomplishments during the internship. Tailoring the resume to highlight relevant experiences gained during the internship enables students to demonstrate their expertise in a particular domain and showcase their contribution to the organization. This not only makes the resume more impactful but also helps in aligning it with the career goals and aspirations of the individual.

Secondly, an updated resume reinforces the importance of continuous professional growth and development. Completing an internship signifies a milestone in a student's journey towards their career path. By updating the resume, students acknowledge the learning experiences and skills acquired during the internship, demonstrating a commitment to self-improvement and the pursuit of excellence in their chosen field.

Moreover, rebuilding the resume reflects adaptability and versatility, two qualities highly valued by potential employers. Internships often provide exposure to different aspects of a job or industry, and capturing these diverse experiences on the resume showcases the student's ability to thrive in varied work environments. This adaptability signals to employers that the student can handle new challenges and contribute effectively to different projects or roles.

In addition, an updated resume helps students stay competitive in the job market. As internship experiences are time-bound, keeping the resume current ensures that students do not miss out on opportunities due to outdated information. In a competitive job market, a well-crafted resume that showcases the most recent experiences and skills can make a significant difference in getting shortlisted for interviews and securing desired positions.

Rebuilding the resume after completing an internship is vital for accurately representing the skills and experiences gained during this valuable learning opportunity. Tailoring the resume to highlight internship-specific achievements showcases the student's expertise and alignment with career goals. Updating the resume reinforces a commitment to continuous growth and adaptability, appealing to potential employers. Moreover, it ensures that the resume remains competitive and up-to-date in the job market, increasing the chances of securing desired job opportunities. By investing time and effort into rebuilding the resume, students can present themselves effectively and make a lasting impression on prospective employers.

Your internship experience is a valuable asset that can significantly enhance your chances of landing your dream job. It showcases your practical skills, industry knowledge, and demonstrates your commitment to professional growth. However, effectively highlighting your internship experience on your resume requires careful thought and strategic planning. In this subchapter, we will explore key strategies to showcase your internship experience on your resume and stand out from the competition.

When preparing a resume post-internship program, there are several important considerations to keep in mind to effectively showcase the newly acquired skills and experiences. The resume after completing an internship should be different from the pre-internship resume to highlight the internship-specific achievements and reflect the individual's growth and development. Here are the key points to consider:

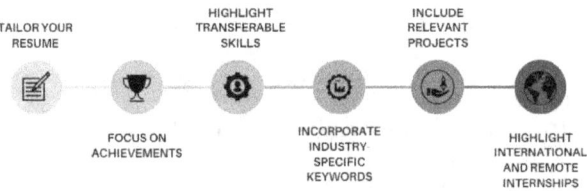

1. **Tailor your resume:** Customize your resume to align with the specific internship or job you are applying for. Highlight the skills and experiences that are most relevant to the position. This will demonstrate your ability to meet the specific requirements of the role and increase your chances of being selected.

2. **Focus on achievements:** Instead of simply listing your duties and responsibilities, emphasize your accomplishments during your internship. Did you contribute to a significant project, receive positive feedback from supervisors, or achieve specific goals? Quantify your achievements whenever possible to provide concrete evidence of your skills and impact.
3. **Highlight transferable skills:** Identify the transferable skills you gained during your internship that are applicable to a wide range of industries. These skills may include communication, teamwork, problem-solving, and time management. Emphasize how these skills can benefit the potential employer and contribute to their organizational success.
4. **Incorporate industry-specific keywords:** Research the keywords and phrases commonly used in the industry you are targeting. Incorporate these keywords throughout your resume to optimize it for applicant tracking systems (ATS) and increase your chances of getting past automated resume screenings.
5. **Include relevant projects:** If you worked on specific projects during your internship that are relevant to the job you are applying for, highlight them. Describe your role, the challenges you faced, and the outcomes

you achieved. This will demonstrate your ability to apply your skills in real-world situations.

6. **Highlight international and remote internships:** If you have completed international or remote internships, make sure to emphasize the unique experiences and skills you gained from such opportunities. These experiences showcase your adaptability, cultural awareness, and ability to work in diverse environments.

Remember, your resume is your marketing tool, and showcasing your internship experience effectively can make all the difference in securing your desired internship or job. By tailoring your resume, focusing on achievements, highlighting transferable skills, incorporating industry-specific keywords, and including relevant projects, you can create a compelling resume that stands out to potential employers.

Whether you are a student, trainee, or aspiring professional in the fields of internships, summer internships, international internships, or remote internships, the strategies outlined in this subchapter will help you to effectively showcase your internship experience on your resume and set you on the path to professional success.

Negotiating Salary and Benefits

The topic of salary negotiation is a vast one - it could practically fill an entire book. While I'm not certain if there's a book solely dedicated to strategies for getting a better salary, just think about how challenging it is to condense such a complex subject into a few paragraphs. Nevertheless, I'll make an attempt to provide some insights and explain why this matter holds significance for you.

At the beginning of this chapter, we discussed the importance of setting the context and understanding the end-to-end process. We also emphasized the significance of salary or compensation in the entire process and why it holds such importance. Now, let's dive one level deeper into the details to gain a better understanding of this matter.

Negotiating your salary and benefits is a critical part of your internship journey. Whether you are a student or trainee, it is vital to recognize your value and stand up for what you deserve. In this subchapter, we will explore effective strategies and helpful tips to guide you through this process, whether you are seeking internships, summer internships, international internships, or remote internships.

First and foremost, research is key. Before entering into any negotiation, gather information about the industry standards and the specific company you are interested in. Understand the market value for interns in your field and the average compensation package. This knowledge will provide you with a solid foundation for your negotiations and enable you to make informed decisions.

Once you have done your research, it is time to assess your own skills, qualifications, and experiences. Identify your unique strengths and how they align with the internship position you are pursuing. This self-assessment will not only boost your confidence but also help you articulate your value proposition during negotiations.

When negotiating, remember to remain professional and confident. Clearly communicate your expectations, emphasizing the value you will bring to the organization. Be prepared to discuss your accomplishments and how they have contributed to your skill development. Additionally, highlight any relevant certifications, coursework, or extracurricular activities that enhance your qualifications.

While salary is important, do not overlook the benefits package. Consider factors such as healthcare, retirement plans, vacation time, and professional development opportunities. These benefits can significantly impact your overall job satisfaction and long-term career growth. If the salary offer does not meet your expectations, negotiating for additional benefits or perks can be an effective alternative.

Furthermore, be open to compromise. Negotiations are a give-and-take process, and it is essential to find a middle ground that satisfies both parties. Be prepared to discuss alternative arrangements, such as flexible working hours or remote work options, which may be mutually beneficial.

Lastly, remember that negotiation is a skill that can be honed through practice. Seek opportunities to practice negotiating, whether it be with friends, mentors, or career services professionals. The more you practice, the more comfortable and confident you will become.

I've always advocated for following best practices and making the right choices. However, life sometimes throws situations at you where you need to be a quick and smart decision-maker. This topic I'm about to discuss holds significance, as I've observed instances where individuals have prioritized their work over their salary for a couple of reasons.

The first reason is a positive one. You might come across an organization that aligns closely with your personal aspirations. It could be a job in your hometown, your favourite company, or a place where your friends work. In such cases, you might happily choose to prioritize your preferences over a higher salary.

The second reason involves situations where you're not able to negotiate a better deal and circumstances force you to accept what's being offered. You might be thinking, "This is the reality most of the time," and you could be right. However, it's important to remember that when people stop compromising, organizations will also stop exploiting.

So, never give up the fight. If not the first time, then maybe the second or third time, you'll be able to negotiate better terms. Keep progressing and believe in yourself.

Chapter 9

Designing Your Own Path: Self-Defined Internship Journey

Aligning Internships with Your Aspirations

I had my doubts about whether to highlight this chapter or not. You might have noticed that I'm not particularly fond of the traditional approach to internships due to the challenges and issues it poses for students. However, I firmly support well-structured internship programs because they play a crucial role in shaping a successful career for upcoming students. And when I refer to a solid internship program, I mean that every individual deserves such a program.

Perhaps this is the reason why it took me a long time to decide and write this chapter. I wanted to ensure that I cover all the important aspects of internships, how to approach them, and what to keep in mind while striving to secure a position in a reputable organization.

I have included valuable insights on how to prepare for interviews, create an impressive resume, and propose yourself effectively to potential employers. However, the reality is that every year, countless students graduate from different programs, and most of them are in dire need of internships to kickstart their careers. But do you think finding internship opportunities is an easy task? And even if they find one, does it truly help them in their career journey, or is it just another checkbox to tick?

In this book, I have discussed the challenges that students face in their search for internships and the importance of finding opportunities that genuinely support their dreams and aspirations. It is crucial to understand that not all internships are created equal, and students deserve internships that truly align with their career goals and offer valuable learning experiences.

So, throughout this chapter, I have endeavoured to shed light on the factors that students should consider while seeking internships and how to make the most out of these opportunities. My aim is to guide and empower students to find internships that can shape their future positively and lead them to the job they truly desire and deserve.

Now, you might be wondering, why on earth did I write this chapter? Well, let me share my reasons, and there are two of them. First, it's based on my own personal experience. Back when I completed my master's degree, I desperately needed a good internship. But back then, the internet wasn't as popular, and social media was probably non-existent. So, I didn't have the exposure or guidance on how to approach a great internship program or how to make the most out of it.

I remember sending out countless applications, hoping someone would take pity on me and offer me an internship. And finally, after a lot of struggles and without much guidance or support, I managed to land an internship. It wasn't anything remarkable, but I thought, "Hey, at least I'm doing something, right?"

Looking back, I realize I had no clue whether what I was doing was right or wrong. I had no idea if I was adding any value or not, and honestly, no one seemed to care either. It was a time when I was just going with the flow, barely knowing if I was on the right track.

After completing my training, I submitted my work, and honestly, I doubt anyone ever read it. No one cared about what I had learned or what my outcome was. Maybe no one even bothered to find out how I spent those two months. It was as if the purpose was just to complete the internship, and get full marks. And that's all that mattered.

Subsequently, I came across a collection of projects, including my own and those of my classmates, tucked away in a corner of the library. To be candid, it didn't trouble me at all. I sensed that the purpose had been fulfilled - I had concluded the internship, obtained approval, and secured my grades. It appeared to be a substantial accomplishment during that period.

But years later, when I had to work really hard to find a job, I realized the true value of internships. Not just any internship, but a good one. I saw how many others, like me, missed out on great internships experience. That's when I realized the need for a self-internship model that could offer exposure, experience, self-learning, and self-development to those who couldn't secure a good internship opportunity.

So, this chapter is dedicated to those students who may not have the chance to experience a fantastic internship. It's about empowering them to create their own self-defined internship, a model that can provide the exposure and learning they deserve for their personal and professional growth. It's time we bridge the gap and ensure that everyone gets the opportunity to unleash their potential through internships, even if they have to pave their own way to do it.

Let's discuss the second reason and also why I felt the need to write this book. Some individuals in the corporate world might not be too thrilled, but it's essential to address these points.

The second reason is based on my own experiences in the corporate world. Throughout my career, I have come across many who approached me for an internship. Even some of my close relatives' children sought internships, but it wasn't as easy as it sounds. I believe many of you might relate to this. Not every organization is open to offering internships, and not everyone enjoys the idea of having interns.

Some organizations have their guidelines and qualification criteria to select candidates for internships. Usually, only top-notch students from reputed colleges get a chance. However, millions of other students are left struggling, trying to find internships. They run from one place to another, seeking any opportunity they can find.

If you find yourself reaching out to relatives and friends for help in securing an internship but receive little or no support in return, it's essential to understand their perspective. It's not that they don't want to support you, but rather that many companies may not be readily accepting interns or considering such requests at the moment. In the corporate world, people are often busy and may have their own priorities and commitments.

Receiving assistance for internships can be challenging as it depends on various factors such as company policies, resource availability, and the current market situation. Not everyone may have the authority or capacity to offer internships or help in securing one. Instead of blaming them, try to empathize with their situation and the challenges they may be facing.

It's crucial to recognize that the corporate world can be highly competitive, and opportunities may not always be readily available. You may need to be persistent and explore multiple avenues to secure an internship that aligns with your interests and career goals.

If someone is unable to help you with your internship search, consider it an opportunity to learn and grow independently. Take charge of your internship journey and look for alternative ways to gain experience and skills. Self-defined internships or other skill-building opportunities can be an excellent way to enhance your resume and stand out to potential employers.

Of course, providing some background was necessary. After all, I wouldn't want to end up like those infamous characters who get bad reputations for no reason! Now, let's get back on track and continue with our original point of discussion.

Today, some students still aspire to do internships because they want to learn and develop skills alongside their studies. They hope to gain valuable experience to boost their future career opportunities. But the truth is, not everyone gets that chance as we know by now. Sometimes, people fail to understand why others don't help them or why they get ignored when seeking internships.

Believe me, there are some stories where people manage to secure internships in corporate settings through unconventional means, but unfortunately, they don't gain much value from such internships. If your internship feels like a "force fit," where there is no genuine commitment from the organization, it can be a frustrating experience. In such cases, you may not be able to derive value from the internship, neither for yourself nor for the company hosting you.

An internship should be a mutually beneficial experience, where you get the opportunity to learn, grow, and contribute to the organization's goals. When the fit is not right, it becomes challenging to align your aspirations and interests with the company's objectives. As a result, you may not gain the practical knowledge and experience that an internship should ideally provide.

The sad reality is that some internships offer little value, leaving the interns disappointed and feeling like they haven't learned much. This is another reason why people shy away from internships. They fear that they might waste their time and effort on something that won't add any value to their lives.

Sometimes, we can't help but feel sorry for those students who want to land a great internship but just can't seem to get it right. It's like they're lost in the internship jungle, with no guide to show them the way. You know those two valuable months of your life that you're supposed to invest in an internship? Well, some end up just passing the time without learning anything substantial. Ah, the genius copy-pasters! They seem to have mastered the art of white-labelling someone else's work and claiming it as their own. You know, those IT interns with their magical library management systems and the finance folks boasting about their "difficult" internship with an accountant. It's quite amusing, don't you think? But hey, let's not be like them. We're here to discover our true potential and create something fresh and unique. So, let's leave the copy-pasting to the "geniuses" and embark on our own journey of self-defined internships!

let's not worry about those who lack the ambition, because we're here to focus on your journey. If you find yourself not getting the support you need, don't fret! That's precisely why I've penned this chapter – to show you there's another path, a self-defined internship that can be even more successful and rewarding than the traditional corporate route.

Sometimes, it feels like students forget why they even joined an internship program in the first place. You know, those "internship in a box" things that colleges and universities offer, where you just fill a form and check the box. They hardly bother to ask what you want to learn or achieve from the internship. It's like they've diluted the whole purpose of internships.

I blame the colleges and universities too. They're not making the situation any better. They just make it seem like some formalities to complete, with deadlines to submit the internship reports. There's no guidance on what to focus on, what value to create, or how to make the most out of the internship. It's like they don't care whether you gain anything valuable from the experience or not.

It's a sad reality for thousands of students out there. They get lost in the mess of internships, with no one to guide them or help them make the most of their time.

Believe me, when I talk about the self-internship program, I feel that it's a powerful approach. It might not have its fancy environment like an actual internship, whether in-person or remote, or even an international one. But despite that, I believe it can deliver a level of value that surpasses many traditional internships. With a self-defined program, the sky's the limit. You know what you can achieve, what you're capable of, and what you truly desire in life.

Certainly, a self-internship program may not cover all aspects comprehensively. However, consider the inspiring examples of successful entrepreneurs who have founded big companies or startups. Take a moment to research their journeys. You'll be surprised to find that many of them didn't rely on traditional internships to achieve their success. Instead, they embraced self-development and pursued innovative ideas that were completely unique, setting them apart from the rest of the world. Their stories demonstrate the power of self-initiative and creativity in shaping remarkable achievements.

In a self-internship program, you focus on finding your objectives and creating a roadmap to achieve them. Instead of reaching out to multiple corporates and sending applications, you invest more time in introspection. You get an excellent opportunity to think deeply about yourself and your future aspirations.

I hope I've instilled a sense of confidence in you that even if you haven't landed a good internship in a corporate setting, you still have a bright future ahead. Creating a self-internship program can be your learning roadmap or a path to self-development that will help you reach your dream job. So, don't be disheartened; take charge of your journey, and create your own path to success!

Alright, we've read a lot of justification today, but let's get a little serious for a moment. For all those students who haven't landed an internship yet, pay close attention to this chapter. Read it carefully and understand how you can design your own self-internship program and follow it to achieve something valuable in your life. It can lead you to that dream job you desire.

So, it's time to begin your journey. Remember, stay focused, stay confident, and believe that this approach will truly help you in your pursuit. Let's take charge of our own destiny and make the most out of every opportunity that comes our way. You've got this!

Let's explore the essential factors you should consider.

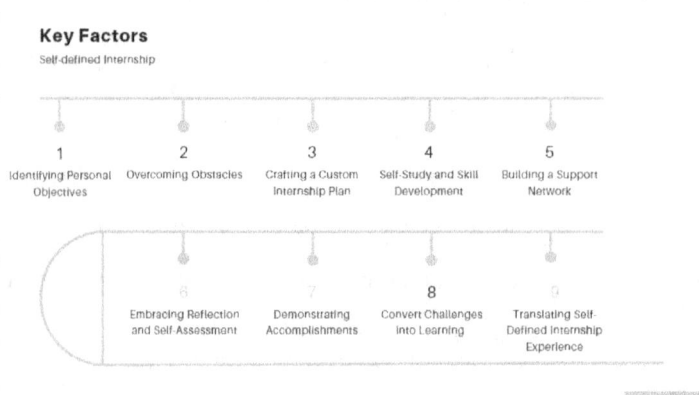

Identifying Personal Objectives

In this crucial section, we delve into the process of identifying your personal objectives for your self-internship program. It's essential to have a clear vision of what you want to achieve and how you can make the most out of this valuable opportunity.

Assessing Career Aspirations and Interests: The first step is to take a deep dive into your career aspirations and interests. Ask yourself the important questions: What field or industry excites you the most? What are your long-term career goals? Understanding your passions and interests will help you align your self-internship program with your future aspirations. It will ensure that you are investing your time and effort in an area that truly matters to you.

Conduct thorough research about different career paths and industries. Explore various roles and job profiles that align with your interests. Talk to professionals working in those fields to gain insights and practical advice. This process of self-assessment will give you clarity on what you genuinely want to achieve and where you want to see yourself in the future.

Setting Clear and Achievable Learning Goals: Once you've identified your career aspirations and interests, the next step is to set clear and achievable learning goals for your self-internship program. These goals act as guideposts, helping you stay focused and on track throughout the journey.

Make sure your learning goals are specific and measurable. Instead of vague objectives like "improve communication skills," be more precise by stating "deliver a presentation to a small group within two months." Break down your goals into smaller milestones, making them more attainable and motivating.

Moreover, ensure that your goals align with your personal interests and career aspirations. This way, you'll be more dedicated to achieving them. Remember that the purpose of your self-internship program is to learn and grow, so set goals that challenge you but are also realistic and achievable within the program's duration.

By clearly defining your career aspirations and setting measurable learning goals, you lay a strong foundation for a successful self-internship program. You'll be better equipped to make the most out of this experience and move closer to your dream job with confidence and determination.

Overcoming Obstacles

In this section, we address the inevitable obstacles that may arise during your self-internship journey. It's essential to be prepared to tackle challenges effectively, as they can shape the course of your learning and personal growth.

Addressing Potential Resource Constraints: One common obstacle you might encounter is resource constraints. Unlike traditional internships, where companies provide resources and support, self-internships require you to be resourceful and creative. You may face limitations in accessing specialized tools, materials, or mentors. However, don't let these constraints discourage you.

To overcome resource limitations, think outside the box. Utilize free online courses, educational platforms, and open-source tools to enhance your learning experience. Network with professionals and industry experts through social media and online forums. Engage in virtual meetups, webinars, and workshops to gain insights and build connections. Remember that the internet is a vast repository of knowledge, and with determination, you can find valuable resources to supplement your self-internship program.

Staying Motivated and Focused Amid Challenges: Another challenge you may encounter is maintaining motivation and focus throughout your self-internship journey. Without the formal structure of a traditional internship, it's easy to lose sight of your goals or get distracted by other commitments.

To stay motivated, create a schedule or timeline for your self-internship program. Set specific milestones and deadlines to track your progress. Regularly review your learning goals and remind yourself why you embarked on this journey in the first place. Celebrate your achievements, no matter how small, to maintain a positive outlook.

Moreover, seek support from friends, family, or mentors who can provide encouragement and feedback. Join virtual study groups or accountability partnerships to stay on track and share experiences with like-minded individuals.

Additionally, remember that self-internships give you the flexibility to adjust your learning path if needed. If you encounter unexpected challenges or feel overwhelmed, take a step back, assess the situation, and modify your approach. Be patient with yourself and trust that every obstacle is an opportunity to grow and learn.

Crafting a Custom Internship Plan

In this section, we dive into the process of creating a custom internship plan tailored to your unique learning objectives and career aspirations. Unlike traditional internships with predefined structures, a self-internship allows you to design a flexible and personalized program that maximizes your learning potential.

Designing a Flexible and Comprehensive Schedule: When crafting your custom internship plan, start by designing a flexible and comprehensive schedule. Consider factors such as your existing commitments, availability, and preferred learning pace. Being flexible allows you to adapt your schedule as needed, ensuring you can balance your self-internship with other responsibilities.

Divide your self-internship program into manageable time blocks, allocating specific periods for research, skill development, and project implementation. Ensure that you set aside sufficient time for reflection and self-assessment to monitor your progress effectively.

Additionally, incorporate breaks and downtime to avoid burnout and maintain overall well-being. A well-balanced schedule will help you stay organized and focused, maximizing the benefits of your self-internship journey.

Defining Project Scope and Milestones for Progress Tracking: Another crucial aspect of crafting your custom internship plan is defining the project scope and setting clear milestones for progress tracking. By outlining specific projects and tasks, you create a roadmap to follow throughout your self-internship.

Break down your projects into smaller, achievable milestones. This approach not only provides a sense of accomplishment but also allows you to monitor your development and adjust your plan if necessary.

Setting milestones also ensures that you stay on track and avoid procrastination. Regularly review your progress and assess whether you are meeting your objectives. If you encounter any challenges, adjust your project scope or seek additional resources to overcome obstacles.

Moreover, tracking your progress allows you to demonstrate your accomplishments in the future. Whether it's for potential employers or further educational pursuits, having a documented record of your achievements will showcase your dedication and commitment to self-improvement.

Self-Study and Skill Development

In this section, we explore the crucial aspects of self-study and skill development during your self-internship journey. As you embark on this path, the opportunities for learning and personal growth are boundless. By actively engaging in self-study and skill development, you can enhance your knowledge, acquire new abilities, and ultimately boost your employability.

Exploring Online Learning Platforms and Courses: One of the key advantages of a self-internship is the freedom to curate your learning experience. Leverage the vast array of online learning platforms and courses available to expand your knowledge in areas of interest or relevance to your career goals.

Explore platforms like Coursera, Udemy, edX, and LinkedIn Learning, among others, which offer courses on a diverse range of subjects, from technical skills to soft skills and beyond. These platforms often provide certification upon course completion, adding value to your resume and showcasing your commitment to continuous learning.

When choosing courses, align them with your internship plan's objectives and the skills you wish to develop. Seek courses that complement your existing knowledge and help you gain expertise in areas relevant to your chosen career path. Remember to pace yourself and focus on absorbing the material effectively.

Seeking Practical Application Opportunities for Skill Building: Self-internships provide the flexibility to practice and apply the skills you learn. To enhance your skill-building journey, seek practical application opportunities that allow you to put your knowledge into practice.

Engage in personal projects, volunteer work, or collaborations with like-minded individuals. For example, if you're studying web development, create a personal website or collaborate with others to build an application. If you're honing your graphic design skills, offer your services to a local organization or start your own design project.

Practical application not only solidifies your understanding but also helps you build a portfolio of real-world projects. This portfolio can be valuable when showcasing your abilities to potential employers or clients.

Moreover, consider seeking mentorship or internships with startups, non-profit organizations, or small businesses, as these environments often offer hands-on experience and mentorship opportunities. The insights gained from working on real projects will further refine your skills and contribute to your overall growth.

Building a Support Network

Within this segment, we explore the significance of establishing a robust support network throughout your self-internship voyage. Constructing meaningful bonds with professors, mentors, fellow students, and online communities can greatly amplify your learning encounter and unveil pathways to invaluable prospects.

Connecting with Professors, Mentors, and Peers: Establishing connections with professors, mentors, and peers is a valuable aspect of your self-internship program. Professors can provide valuable guidance, share industry insights, and offer feedback on your progress. They can also serve as references when you apply for future opportunities.

Seek out mentors who have expertise in your chosen field or career path. Mentors can offer valuable advice, share their own experiences, and provide constructive feedback on your work. They can be instrumental in helping you navigate challenges and make informed decisions.

Additionally, building a network of like-minded peers can be mutually beneficial. Share your experiences, collaborate on projects, and support each other's growth. Engaging with peers can foster a sense of camaraderie and provide a platform for exchanging ideas and knowledge.

Leveraging Virtual Communities and Networking Platforms:

In the digital age, virtual communities and networking platforms have become powerful tools for connecting with professionals and enthusiasts worldwide. Platforms like LinkedIn, professional forums, and social media groups allow you to interact with individuals from various industries and geographical locations.

Joining relevant virtual communities can expose you to diverse perspectives, industry trends, and valuable resources. Actively participate in discussions, share your insights, and seek advice from experienced professionals. Virtual networking opens doors to potential collaborations, freelance opportunities, and even job openings.

Additionally, virtual networking events and webinars provide opportunities to connect with industry experts and thought leaders. Participating in these events allows you to expand your network and gain insights from successful individuals who have navigated their career paths.

Remember, building a support network is a two-way street. Be proactive in reaching out, offering help, and showing genuine interest in others' endeavours. Authentic relationships are built on mutual respect and a willingness to contribute to each other's growth.

By cultivating a robust support network of professors, mentors, peers, and virtual communities, you can access a wealth of knowledge, inspiration, and support throughout your self-internship journey. These connections can play a pivotal role in shaping your learning experience, guiding your decisions, and propelling you toward success in your future endeavours.

Embracing Reflection and Self-Assessment

In this section, we explore the significance of reflection and self-assessment as integral components of your self-internship program. By cultivating a growth mindset and actively seeking feedback, you can harness valuable insights that drive continuous improvement and personal development.

Cultivating a Growth Mindset and Embracing Feedback:

Adopting a growth mindset is the foundation of successful self-internship experiences. Embrace the belief that your abilities can be developed through dedication and hard work.

Understand that challenges and setbacks are opportunities for learning and growth, not indicators of failure.

Seeking feedback is a crucial aspect of personal development. Embrace constructive criticism as a tool to refine your skills and work on areas that need improvement. Actively ask for feedback from mentors, professors, and peers, and be receptive to their insights. Embracing feedback with an open mind demonstrates a commitment to self-improvement and helps you build resilience in the face of challenges.

Moreover, be proactive in soliciting feedback from those you collaborate with during your self-internship. Regularly seeking input on your projects and ideas can lead to valuable suggestions and fresh perspectives, enriching your learning experience.

Regularly Reflecting on Achievements and Challenges: Reflection is a powerful tool for personal growth and learning. Take time to regularly reflect on your achievements and challenges during your self-internship journey. Celebrate your successes and acknowledge your progress, as this can boost your motivation and confidence.

On the other hand, analyzing your challenges and setbacks can lead to valuable insights and new strategies for improvement. Reflect on what worked well and what could be done differently in various aspects of your self-internship, such as time management, skill development, and project execution.

To facilitate effective reflection, consider maintaining a journal or digital log to record your thoughts, experiences, and discoveries. Track your accomplishments, highlight key learnings, and identify areas where you can enhance your skills.

Use reflection as an opportunity for self-assessment. Set aside dedicated time to evaluate your growth, identify areas of strength, and pinpoint areas where you can continue to develop. Create actionable goals based on your reflections and design a plan for future improvement.

Demonstrating Accomplishments

In this section, we delve into the significance of showcasing your accomplishments effectively during your self-internship program. Demonstrating your skills and achievements through a well-crafted portfolio or project showcase and leveraging online platforms can significantly enhance your visibility and outreach to potential employers or collaborators.

Creating an Impressive Portfolio or Project Showcase:

A compelling portfolio or project showcase is a powerful tool to exhibit your capabilities, creativity, and achievements. Include a diverse range of projects, assignments, and initiatives that showcase your skills, problem-solving abilities, and accomplishments throughout your self-internship journey.

Craft a visually appealing and organized portfolio that highlights your best work. Use clear and concise descriptions to explain the objectives of each project, your role, and the impact of your contributions. Consider incorporating multimedia elements such as images, videos, and interactive content to make your portfolio engaging and memorable.

A well-structured portfolio provides a comprehensive overview of your abilities and leaves a lasting impression on potential employers or collaborators. It serves as tangible evidence of your capabilities and showcases your dedication to personal and professional growth.

Utilizing Online Platforms for Visibility and Outreach:

In today's digital age, online platforms offer unparalleled opportunities to increase your visibility and reach a wider audience. Create a professional presence on platforms and regularly update them with your latest projects and accomplishments.

LinkedIn, in particular, is a powerful networking tool that connects professionals across various industries. Use it to highlight your self-internship experiences, share insightful articles or blog posts, and engage with industry influencers. Building a strong online network can lead to valuable connections and potential job or collaboration opportunities.

Additionally, consider creating a personal website or blog where you can showcase your portfolio, share your self-internship journey, and demonstrate your expertise in your chosen field. Regularly update your website with fresh content, relevant achievements, and industry-related insights to keep your audience engaged.

Leverage social media platforms to amplify your reach and connect with like-minded individuals or organizations. Share your work, insights, and successes across platforms like Twitter, Instagram, or Facebook to expand your online presence and garner more visibility.

By effectively utilizing online platforms, you can showcase your accomplishments to a global audience and position yourself as a proactive, talented, and innovative individual. Creating a compelling online presence can significantly enhance your professional prospects and open doors to exciting opportunities within your chosen field.

Transforming Challenges into Learning Opportunities

In this section, we explore the importance of embracing challenges during your self-internship program and using them as valuable learning opportunities. Adapting to unexpected situations and transforming failures into lessons for personal growth are essential skills that can propel your development and success.

Adapting to Unexpected Situations and Change: Throughout your self-internship journey, you may encounter unexpected situations, setbacks, or changes in your plans. Rather than viewing these challenges as obstacles, embrace them as opportunities for growth and learning.

Adaptability is a crucial skill in any professional setting, and self-internship provides an excellent opportunity to hone this skill. Learn to remain flexible and open-minded in the face of uncertainty. Approach unforeseen circumstances with a positive mindset and a willingness to find creative solutions.

Remember that unexpected challenges can often lead to unforeseen opportunities. By staying resilient and adaptable, you can turn these challenges into chances to demonstrate your resourcefulness and ability to thrive in diverse situations.

Transforming Failures into Lessons for Personal Growth:

Failure is an inevitable part of any learning journey, including self-internship. Instead of being discouraged by failures, view them as valuable learning experiences that can contribute to your personal growth and development.

When you encounter failures or setbacks, take the time to reflect on the reasons behind them. Identify the areas where you can improve and use these insights to refine your approach. Embrace a growth mindset, where failures are seen as stepping stones toward improvement rather than indicators of inadequacy.

Use failures as opportunities to build resilience and perseverance. Each setback offers a chance to reassess your goals, refine your strategies, and emerge stronger and wiser. Share your experiences and learnings with others, as it can inspire and motivate them to overcome their challenges too.

By embracing challenges and failures as learning opportunities, you cultivate a growth-oriented mindset that fosters continuous improvement. This approach not only enhances your self-internship experience but also equips you with valuable skills that are highly regarded in the professional world. As you embrace these challenges and transform them into learning opportunities, you build a solid foundation for personal and professional success in the long run.

Translating Self-Defined Internship Experience

In this section, we focus on the crucial aspect of effectively communicating your self-defined internship experience to potential employers. Articulating your journey in job applications and interviews is essential to demonstrate the value and relevance of your self-internship experience to your future career aspirations.

Articulating the Journey in Job Applications and Interviews:

When applying for jobs or attending interviews, it is vital to effectively convey your self-defined internship experience to prospective employers. The challenge lies in presenting your unique learning journey in a way that highlights its significance and aligns with the requirements of the position you are seeking.

Begin by crafting a well-structured resume that emphasizes your self-internship experience, showcasing the skills and knowledge you acquired during the process. Tailor your resume to align with the specific job description, emphasizing how your self-internship journey has prepared you for the role.

During interviews, confidently articulate your self-internship experience, focusing on the challenges you encountered, the projects you undertook, and the skills you developed. Highlight how your self-driven initiative, adaptability, and problem-solving abilities make you a valuable candidate.

Relating Skills Gained to Future Career Aspirations: To make the most of your self-defined internship experience, you must connect the skills and knowledge you gained to your future career aspirations. Identify the transferrable skills and competencies you developed during your self-internship that are relevant to your desired career path.

Whether it's leadership, communication, analytical thinking, or project management, demonstrate how your self-internship journey has equipped you with these skills. Provide concrete examples of how you applied these skills during your self-internship projects, as well as how they align with the requirements of your target job role.

By effectively relating the skills gained through your self-internship to your future career aspirations, you present yourself as a well-rounded and proactive candidate.

Employers appreciate candidates who take initiative and actively seek opportunities for self-improvement and growth.

Translating your self-defined internship experience is essential to make a lasting impression on potential employers. Articulating your journey effectively in job applications and interviews, along with relating the skills gained to your future career aspirations, enhances your credibility and marketability as a professional. By showcasing the value of your self-internship experience, you increase your chances of landing your dream job and embarking on a successful career journey.

In this chapter, we've explored what self-internship is and how it can be made successful. Taking charge of your own learning and staying focused on your personal objectives can empower you with confidence and a unique experience, setting you apart from others in the corporate world. Despite facing challenges, you can navigate and stay motivated by yourself.

I hope you've read this chapter carefully and understood its details. The message I've been trying to convey is to stay motivated and overcome any obstacles that come your way. With determination, you can complete your self-defined internship and showcase it as a serious effort to your college and university, gaining recognition in the corporate world beyond what a normal intern achieves.

Before wrapping up this chapter, I want to stress the importance of seeking continuous feedback for your self-defined internship. Regular feedback helps you stay on the right track and make necessary adjustments. As you embark on this journey, consider having a coach or mentor by your side to provide guidance and support.

Chapter 10

Creating a Long-Term Career Development Plan

When you embark on your internship preparations, it's crucial not to view it simply as a short-term task that lasts for a couple of months. An internship serves as your entryway into the corporate world and lays the foundation for your long-term career growth. Recognize that an internship holds significant importance, allowing you to dip your toes into the professional realm and begin your journey toward lasting career development.

Your internship experience goes beyond a mere assignment; it's a valuable opportunity to explore the broader landscape. It's like testing the waters before crafting your own unique path. Make the most of your internship by gaining insights into your strengths, identifying your areas of interest, determining the industry you're drawn to, and pinpointing the regions that offer the most growth potential. Throughout your internship, you'll assess your choices while actively engaging in your assigned tasks. This period of hands-on experience helps you refine your focus and shape your career aspirations.

I've observed numerous students who, after undergoing internships, have altered their plans of pursuing corporate jobs. Instead, some have chosen to initiate their own startups, while others opt to continue family businesses. By now, you likely comprehend the underlying factors that contribute to these decisions. An internship serves as a platform to establish the trajectory of your future endeavours. It enables you to assess various aspects and make informed adjustments, steering your course towards long-term career development.

I would like to continue to address one of the factors that lead students to opt out of pursuing a corporate career, and it's essential to wrap up this discussion, particularly the "why" aspect. There are significant reasons behind students choosing to embark on their own startup ventures or to continue with family businesses or do nothing after completing an internship. I've categorized these reasons into two distinct categories.

In one category, there are students or participants who have a clear vision for their future plans. They view internships as a platform to enhance their understanding, gain insights into the corporate world, grasp the nuances of business operations, and interact with individuals of diverse personalities. This experience cultivates a new attitude and personality that can prove valuable, even if they choose to continue with their family business. It's noteworthy that students hailing from strong family business backgrounds are already familiar with the business landscape due to their exposure and involvement in supporting or observing family members like fathers, uncles, elder siblings managing the business. Their familiarity with the business world, gained long before embarking on their professional internships, essentially acts as stepping stones, propelling them into their own family business ventures.

Now, let's delve into the second category. This category pertains to those students who share a common objective with many others: to complete an internship and secure a decent job. However, for these students, their internship experience might not have been as successful or professional as they had hoped. Consequently, they may have developed reservations about entering the job market, apprehensive about working under someone else. Various reasons can contribute to this perception, creating a sense of unease or a lack of readiness to embrace their future career growth journey. It's important to note that one of the key motivations behind writing this book is to assist such students in improving their internship approach, strategizing effectively, and executing their plans more efficiently. By doing so, they can achieve outcomes that guide them onto a successful career path. The entirety of this book is centred around addressing the needs of this particular category of students.

Coming back to our original thread, the dynamics of career transitions have evolved over time. In the past, it was relatively common for individuals to switch industries or completely shift their skillsets. However, this traditional approach often led to a disruption in the momentum of personal growth. Not everyone is fortunate enough to seamlessly navigate such transitions while maintaining a steady trajectory.

Undoubtedly, these shifts can be risky endeavours, often endangering the progression you've achieved thus far. Transitioning to a new industry or role requires starting anew, essentially rebuilding your value and reputation from scratch. Frequent and abrupt changes early in your career can potentially impede your growth.

It's worth noting that as you mature and gain experience within an industry, your attitude and personality become key drivers of change. However, for newcomers or those with limited exposure, such abrupt shifts can prove detrimental to your overall career advancement.

The occurrence of such a mindset shift within the initial two to three years of your career is not uncommon, as I mentioned earlier. This tendency often stems from not fully leveraging your internship experience to ascertain your post-study aspirations. It's crucial to recognize that internships should not be pursued merely for the sake of completing them; rather, they should serve as a compass to guide your journey toward long-term career development.

Consider your internship as a pivotal life event, one that has the potential to shape your future trajectory. Now, let's delve into how you can harness this opportunity effectively and outline the essential steps for better planning.

Assessing Your Skills, Interests, and Values

It is crucial for interns to have a clear understanding of their skills, interests, and values. By assessing these key aspects, you can effectively navigate the internship landscape and pave your path to professional success. This subchapter will guide you through the process of self-assessment, helping you identify your strengths, passions, and what truly matters to you.

Skills assessment is the first step towards finding the right internship. Take the time to evaluate your academic achievements, extracurricular activities, and any relevant work experience. Identify the areas where you excel and the skills you have developed, such as communication, problem-solving, or leadership. Understanding your abilities will enable you to target internships that align with your strengths and provide opportunities for growth.

Next, delve into your interests. What subjects or industries ignite your curiosity? Are you passionate about technology, art, social justice, or business? Make a list of your interests and explore how they can be translated into potential internship opportunities. Remember, internships are not only about gaining experience but also about pursuing your passions and exploring future career paths.

Equally important is assessing your values. What are the ethical principles and beliefs that guide your decision-making? Do you value diversity, sustainability, or community engagement? Understanding your values will help you find internships that align with your personal and professional goals, ensuring a fulfilling experience that resonates with who you are as an individual.

Once you have assessed your skills, interests, and values, it's time to research internship opportunities that match your criteria. Whether you are seeking a summer internship, an international experience, or a remote opportunity, there are countless options available. Look for internships that provide an environment where you can further develop your skills, explore your interests, and contribute to causes that matter to you.

Remember, self-assessment is an ongoing process. As you gain more experience and insights, your skills, interests, and values may evolve. Embrace this growth and continue to assess yourself periodically, ensuring that you are on the right track towards professional success.

In summary, assessing your skills, interests, and values is an essential step in mapping out your internship roadmap. By gaining clarity on these aspects, you can identify opportunities that align with your strengths, passions, and values. So, take the time to self-reflect, research, and explore various internship options. Remember, the right internship can be a transformative experience, propelling you towards a successful career.

Setting Long-Term Career Goals

It is crucial for students and interns to not only excel in their current internships but also to have a clear vision for their long-term career goals. By setting long-term career goals, you can map out a path to professional success and ensure that your internships align with your ultimate aspirations. In this subchapter, we will explore the importance of setting long-term career goals and provide practical steps to help you define and pursue your desired career path.

The Significance of Long-Term Career Goals:

- Long-term career goals provide a sense of direction and purpose, helping you make informed decisions about internships and other professional opportunities.
- They serve as a roadmap for your career journey, helping you stay focused and motivated to achieve your aspirations.
- Setting long-term career goals enables you to prioritize your efforts, allocate resources effectively, and make the most of your internships.

Defining Your Long-Term Career Goals:

- Reflect on your passions, interests, and skills to identify areas of professional interest. Research different industries and job roles to gain a better understanding of potential career paths.
- Consider your values and what you want to achieve in your career, both personally and professionally.
- Set specific, measurable, achievable, relevant, and time-bound (SMART) goals that resonate with your aspirations.

Pursuing Your Long-Term Career Goals:

- Break down your long-term goals into smaller, manageable short-term goals.
- Seek out internships that align with your long-term career goals, whether they are in your desired industry, location, or field of interest.
- Take advantage of summer internships, international internships, and remote internships to gain diverse experiences and broaden your skill set.
- Network with professionals in your desired field, attend career fairs, and participate in mentorship programs to expand your industry connections.

- Continually evaluate and adjust your goals as your interests and priorities evolve throughout your internship journey.

To sum up, setting long-term career goals is essential for students and interns embarking on internships. By defining your aspirations and aligning your internships with those goals, you can maximize your professional growth and pave the way for future success. Remember, internships are not only about gaining experience but also about shaping your career trajectory. So, take the time to set long-term career goals and design your internship roadmap accordingly.

Identifying Professional Development Opportunities

As an interns, embarking on an internship is a crucial step towards launching a successful professional career. However, the journey doesn't stop at securing an internship position. In fact, it is just the beginning. To make the most out of your internship experience, it is essential to identify and seize professional development opportunities that align with your goals and aspirations. This subchapter aims to guide and equip you with the necessary tools to identify these opportunities.

This book recognizes that internships come in various forms, including summer internships, international internships, remote internships, and Self-defined. Regardless of the type, the principles for identifying professional development opportunities remain universally applicable.

The first step in identifying these opportunities is self-reflection. Understand your strengths, weaknesses, and areas of interest. What skills do you want to develop during your internship? Reflecting on these questions will help you narrow down the specific areas you want to focus on during your professional development journey.

Next, research the organization or company hosting your internship. Familiarize yourself with their vision, mission, and values. By understanding their objectives, you can align your professional development goals with theirs. Look for opportunities within the organization that will allow you to contribute to their mission while enhancing your skills and knowledge.

Networking is another crucial aspect of identifying professional development opportunities. Engage with your supervisors, colleagues, and even fellow interns. Attend company events, workshops, and seminars. Building relationships with professionals in your field will not only expand your network but could also open doors to new opportunities for growth and development.

Additionally, leverage online resources and platforms to discover industry-specific training programs, webinars, and conferences. Many organizations offer online courses or certifications that can enhance your skillset and boost your resume. Take advantage of these resources to stay up-to-date with the latest industry trends and developments.

Lastly, be proactive in seeking feedback and guidance from your mentors and supervisors. Regularly schedule check-ins to discuss your progress and areas for improvement. This feedback will provide valuable insights into areas where you can further develop your skills.

Remember, identifying professional development opportunities is an ongoing process. As your internship progresses, continuously evaluate your goals and adjust your strategies accordingly. By embracing these opportunities, you are paving the way for a successful and fulfilling professional career.

Building a Strong Professional Network

Building a strong professional network is essential for students and interns looking to kickstart their careers. Whether you are pursuing an internship, summer internship, international internship, or remote internship, having a robust network can open doors to countless opportunities and pave the way for professional success. This subchapter will guide you through the steps necessary to develop and nurture a network that will support your aspirations.

The first step in building a strong professional network is to identify your goals and target industries. Determine the areas you are passionate about and where you envision yourself working in the future. Research organizations, companies, and professionals within those industries and make a list of individuals who could potentially become valuable connections.

Once you have identified your target network, it is crucial to engage actively and cultivate relationships. Attend industry events, conferences, and job fairs where you can meet professionals and fellow interns who share your interests. Actively participate in online communities, forums, and social media groups related to your field. This will allow you to connect with like-minded individuals and expand your network beyond geographical boundaries.

Networking should not be limited to formal events. Take advantage of informal settings, such as coffee chats, informational interviews, and networking lunches, to build genuine connections with professionals. Approach these interactions with a genuine curiosity and desire to learn from others' experiences. Remember, networking is a two-way street, and offering value to others through your knowledge or skills will strengthen your connections.

Maintaining and nurturing your network is equally important. Regularly stay in touch with your contacts through emails, LinkedIn messages, or occasional meet-ups. Share relevant articles, industry updates, or job opportunities that might interest them. Participate in mentorship programs or seek guidance from experienced professionals who can provide valuable insights and advice.

Lastly, always remember to express gratitude and reciprocate the support you receive from your network. Show appreciation by acknowledging the help and guidance you receive from your connections. Be willing to offer assistance whenever possible, providing value to your network in return.

Building a strong professional network takes time and effort, but it is an investment that will pay off in the long run. By developing genuine connections, actively engaging with professionals, and nurturing those relationships, you will enhance your internship experience and set yourself up for future success.

Continuously Evolving and Adapting in Your Career

The ability to evolve and adapt is crucial for success in any career. As students, it is important to recognize that your career journey is not a linear path but rather a dynamic and evolving process. The subchapter aims to equip you with the necessary mindset and skills to navigate the ever-changing landscape of internships and beyond.

Internships serve as an excellent platform to gain practical experience and develop essential skills. However, it is essential to understand that internships are not just about completing tasks assigned to you, but also about learning and growing as a professional. As you embark on your internship journey, it is crucial to adopt a growth mindset and embrace opportunities for personal and professional development.

One way to continuously evolve in your career is by seeking out diverse experiences. Consider exploring different types of internships such as summer internships, international internships, or remote internships. Each of these niches offers unique advantages and challenges, enabling you to broaden your skill set and adapt to different working environments. By stepping out of your comfort zone and embracing new experiences, you can enhance your adaptability and increase your marketability in the job market.

Another aspect of continuously evolving and adapting in your career is staying updated with industry trends and technological advancements. The world is changing at an unprecedented pace, and it is crucial to stay ahead of the curve. Actively seek out opportunities to learn about emerging technologies, attend workshops, and engage with industry professionals. By staying updated, you can position yourself as a valuable asset to any organization, demonstrating your ability to adapt to new ways of working.

Plus, building a strong professional network is crucial for career growth. Attend networking events, connect with professionals in your field of interest, and seek mentors who can guide you along your career path. Your network can provide valuable insights, open doors to new opportunities, and support your growth and development.

In summary, the subchapter emphasizes the importance of embracing change and proactively seeking growth opportunities. By adopting a growth mindset, seeking diverse experiences, staying updated with industry trends, and building a strong professional network, you can navigate the ever-changing landscape of internships and position yourself for long-term professional success. Remember, your career is a journey, and it is up to you to continuously evolve and adapt along the way.

Conclusion: Your Path to Professional Success

As we come to the end of this book, it is crucial to reflect on the knowledge and insights gained throughout your journey. The internship roadmap you have followed has provided you with the necessary tools and guidance to navigate the complex terrain of professional success. Whether you are a student or a trainee, this conclusion marks a new beginning for you in your quest to achieve your career goals.

Internships are a pivotal stepping stone towards professional success. They offer a unique opportunity for students and interns to gain practical experience, develop essential skills, and build a strong network. By participating in internships, you have taken a proactive approach towards shaping your future. You have recognized the value of hands-on learning and have embraced the challenges and opportunities that come with it.

Summer internships, international internships, and remote internships have all been explored in this book, highlighting the diverse range of options available to you. These experiences have the power to broaden your horizons, exposing you to new cultures, industries, and ways of working. By stepping outside of your comfort zone, you have demonstrated adaptability and a willingness to embrace change – qualities highly valued in today's dynamic job market.

As you embark on your path to professional success, remember that the journey is not linear. It is filled with twists and turns, setbacks and triumphs. Embrace each experience as a stepping stone towards your ultimate goal. Stay resilient in the face of challenges and maintain a growth mindset. Seek out mentors who can guide and inspire you along the way. Build relationships with your peers and colleagues, as they will become an invaluable support system throughout your career.

Furthermore, continue to invest in your personal and professional development. Take advantage of opportunities for continued learning, whether it be through workshops, seminars, or online courses. Stay up-to-date with industry trends and advancements, as this will enable you to remain competitive and adaptable in an ever-evolving job market.

Ultimately, your path to professional success lies in your hands. The internship roadmap you have followed has provided you with the necessary tools and insights to navigate this journey. Embrace the challenges, seize the opportunities, and never stop learning and growing. With determination, resilience, and a clear vision of your goals, you are well on your way to achieving professional success.

"Success is not the key to happiness. Happiness is the key to success. If you love what you are doing, you will be successful."

By Albert Schweitzer

Extended Content

Additional Resources for Internship Success

In the present day, students are exceptionally capable and high in energy. They just require proper guidance and direction to surpass the achievements of past generations. I firmly believe that the current generation is brimming with energy and unmatched ambition. If shown even a small path, I am convinced that they can achieve something significant in their lives. With this very intention, I have authored this book. We have journeyed through the book's contents and come to its conclusion. However, I recognized that there are numerous students who might not have extensive exposure to the internet and social media, and they too deserve assistance. For this reason, I deemed it necessary to extend further guidance to them.

I want to convey to you that when you are preparing for your internship, ensure that you explore online platforms. Visit various platforms where internship opportunities are posted.

In today's date, numerous online portals and platforms are available that connect you with corporate organizations. They make an effort to provide you with internship opportunities relevant to your skills. Sometimes these internships are paid, and sometimes they are not. Nevertheless, these platforms exist to help you streamline your efforts and save time that might otherwise be spent extensively researching.

Building a network and connecting with people is crucial for your internship preparation and future prospects. We've talked about this topic multiple times, and I'm sure you're becoming skilled at networking. There are various platforms accessible to you that can help you become a part of a professional network. You see, you never know when a job opportunity aligned with your aspirations might arise from your professional connections. I'll provide a summary of this again for you in this chapter.

Lastly, a critical aspect to consider is ensuring your readiness, especially when your internship involves specialized skills that require prior training. This becomes particularly important when certain organizations have high expectations, and the internship duration is relatively short. It's natural that you want to both learn and perform effectively during your internship. To better equip yourself, online courses and development programs can be tremendously beneficial. These courses offer foundational knowledge before you embark on your internship journey.

For instance, if you're aiming to pursue an internship in the technology field, and your goal is to become a successful developer or programmer in the future, enrolling in a basic programming language course like Python or C++ could provide you with a valuable head start. This extra preparation through online courses can give you an advantageous edge as you begin your internship.

While I'm providing you with additional tools to enhance your chances of success, I want to stress the need to remain aware of potential scams or fraudulent activities in the market. Unfortunately, there are individuals who may try to take advantage of your situation, offering false promises or charging exorbitant fees for securing internships.

Being cautious is extremely important, especially if someone is asking you to pay for an internship opportunity. In the professional realm, respected organizations and companies typically don't ask interns to pay for a legitimate internship position. Unfortunately, there are individuals out there with questionable intentions who are primarily focused on their own interests, not your career goals or well-being.

While keeping your motivation high, I also urge you to stay vigilant. Conduct thorough research, confirm the legitimacy of any offers, and trust your instincts. Your career path holds significant value, and your efforts should be directed towards opportunities that genuinely contribute to your personal growth and progress.

Now, let's circle back to the resources that can aid you in securing and excelling in your internship journey.

Internship Search Websites and Platforms

In today's competitive job market, internship search websites and platforms come into play, serving as a valuable tool in your quest for the ideal internship.

Internship search platforms act as a centralized hub, connecting aspiring interns with a wide range of internship opportunities. These platforms offer a user-friendly interface that allows students and interns to search for internships based on their preferences, including location, industry, duration, and more. Whether you are looking for a summer internship, an international experience, or even a remote internship, these platforms cater to various niches, making the search process efficient and tailored to your specific needs.

Summer internships are highly sought-after by students, as they provide the perfect opportunity to gain hands-on experience during the break from academic studies. Internship search websites and platforms curate a vast array of summer internships across different industries, allowing you to explore options and make informed decisions about the best fit for you. These platforms often provide additional resources such as interview tips, resume builders, and networking opportunities to enhance your chances of securing your dream summer internship.

For those seeking international internships, online website and platforms offer a gateway to incredible opportunities around the globe. Whether you aspire to work in a bustling metropolis or immerse yourself in a different culture, internship search websites and platforms provide access to internships in various countries and regions. International internships not only offer professional growth but also foster personal development, as you navigate new environments and expand your global network.

The rise of remote work has opened up a new realm of internship possibilities. Remote internships allow students and interns to gain practical experience from the comfort of their own homes. Internship search websites and platforms provide a wide range of remote internship opportunities across diverse industries, ensuring that geographical constraints do not hinder your professional growth.

In conclusion, when embarking on your internship search journey, make sure to utilize the power of internship search websites and platforms. These invaluable resources cater to the needs of students and interns, offering a streamlined and efficient process to find internships that align with your interests, whether it be summer internships, international experiences, or remote work opportunities. By leveraging these platforms, you can map out your path to professional success and pave the way for a fulfilling and rewarding internship experience.

Professional Associations and Networking Events

One of the most valuable aspects of an internship is the opportunity to connect with professionals in your field and expand your network. Building strong relationships with individuals who share similar interests and goals can open doors to future career opportunities and provide valuable insights and guidance along the way. Professional associations and networking events offer the perfect platform for students and interns to engage with industry experts and like-minded individuals.

Professional associations are organizations that bring together professionals from a specific industry or field. These associations provide a range of resources and benefits to their members, including access to industry-specific information, networking opportunities, and professional development programs. By joining a professional association related to your internship or desired career path, you can gain exposure to the latest industry trends, connect with experienced professionals, and stay informed about job opportunities. Additionally, many associations offer mentorship programs, where seasoned professionals provide guidance and support to help you navigate your internship and future career.

Attending networking events is another effective way to expand your professional network. These events bring together professionals from various industries, allowing you to meet new people, exchange ideas, and potentially form valuable connections. Whether it's a local meet-up, a conference, or a career fair, networking events provide a platform to showcase your skills and interests, learn from industry leaders, and explore internship opportunities.

For students seeking summer internships, professional associations often host job fairs or offer online platforms where companies specifically recruit interns. These events provide a unique chance to interact directly with recruiters and learn about internship programs tailored to your field of interest. Additionally, many associations offer workshops or seminars specifically designed to help students enhance their internship applications and interview skills.

In the era of remote work and international internships, professional associations and networking events have adapted to the digital landscape. Online platforms, such as virtual conferences and webinars, allow students and interns to connect with professionals from around the world without geographical limitations. These virtual networking opportunities provide the chance to engage with industry leaders, learn about global trends, and potentially secure remote or international internships.

In the end, professional associations and networking events are essential resources for students and interns pursuing internships. By actively engaging with these platforms, you can expand your professional network, gain industry insights, and increase your chances of securing meaningful internship experiences. Whether you are participating in summer internships, international internships, or remote internships, professional associations and networking events are valuable tools in your journey to professional success.

Online Courses and Skill Development Platforms

It has become increasingly important for students and interns to acquire the necessary skills and knowledge to stay competitive in the job market. Traditional methods of learning, such as classroom-based education, may not always provide the flexibility and specialization needed to keep up with the demands of the industry. This is where online courses and skill development platforms come into play.

Online courses offer a wide range of benefits for students and interns, particularly those seeking internships, summer internships, international internships, and remote internships. These platforms provide a convenient and accessible way to gain valuable skills and knowledge, all from the comfort of your own home. Whether you're looking to enhance your technical abilities, develop soft skills, or gain industry-specific knowledge, there is an online course available to cater to your needs.

One of the major advantages of online courses is their flexibility. Unlike traditional classroom-based education, online courses allow you to learn at your own pace and on your own schedule. This is especially beneficial for students and interns who are juggling multiple commitments, such as part-time jobs or other extracurricular activities. With online courses, you have the freedom to set your own learning hours, making it easier to balance your internship requirements with your personal life.

Moreover, online courses offer a wide range of subjects and specializations, ensuring that you can find a course that aligns with your career aspirations and interests. From coding and digital marketing to project management and leadership skills, the options are virtually limitless. By enrolling in these courses, you can acquire valuable skills that will not only enhance your resume but also make you a more attractive candidate for internships.

Online courses often provide opportunities for networking and collaboration. Many platforms have discussion forums, where students and interns can interact with instructors and peers from around the world. This allows you to connect with like-minded individuals, share ideas, and gain insights from professionals in the field. These connections can be invaluable when it comes to finding internship opportunities or even securing a job in the future.

To conclude, online courses and skill development platforms offer a wealth of opportunities for students and interns looking to enhance their skills and knowledge. Whether you're interested in internships, summer internships, international internships, or remote internships, online courses provide a flexible and accessible way to gain the skills needed to succeed in today's competitive job market. So, why wait? Start exploring the vast range of online courses available and take your first step towards professional success.

Thank You

I am deeply grateful for your time and attention in reading my book on the *"Internship Roadmap: Mapping Out Your Path to Professional Success."* It brings me immense joy to know that you took an interest in exploring the world of internships and career development through these pages.

My primary goal in writing this book was to provide valuable insights and guidance to college graduates like you, embarking on their journey towards a successful internship experience. I hope that you found the content informative, practical, and easy to understand, tailored specifically to your needs.

As you progress in your career, I sincerely hope that you will be able to leverage the tips, techniques, and best practices shared in this book to make the most out of your internship opportunities. Whether it's crafting an impressive resume and cover letter, acing interviews, or addressing common challenges, I believe that the knowledge you've gained will serve as a valuable resource on your path to professional growth.

Remember, each internship is an opportunity to learn, grow, and develop both personally and professionally. Embrace every challenge, seize every chance to showcase your skills, and be proactive in seeking feedback and continuous improvement.

Lastly, I encourage you to share your learnings with others, as knowledge shared is knowledge multiplied. Let this book be a source of inspiration for your peers, friends, and colleagues as they embark on their internship journeys too.

Thank you once again for being a part of this journey with me. Your support and readership mean the world to me. I wish you the best of luck in your future endeavours, and may you make the most of every internship opportunity that comes your way.

Here's to your success and a bright future!

"The journey of a thousand miles begins with a single step."

By Maya Thompson

www.ingramcontent.com/pod-product-compliance
Lightning Source LLC
Chambersburg PA
CBHW052146220526

45471CB00004B/1553